How
BRAIN SCIENCE
CAN MAKE YOU A
BETTER LAWYER

HOW
BRAIN SCIENCE
CAN MAKE YOU A
BETTER LAWYER

DAVID A. SOUSA

AMERICAN BAR ASSOCIATION
**Defending Liberty
Pursuing Justice**

Cover design by ABA Publishing

The materials contained herein represent the opinions of the authors and editors and should not be construed to be the action of the American Bar Association unless adopted pursuant to the bylaws of the Association.

Nothing contained in this book is to be considered as the rendering of legal advice for specific cases, and readers are responsible for obtaining such advice from their own legal counsel. This book and any forms and agreements herein are intended for educational and informational purposes only.

Printed in the United States of America.

13 12 11 10 09   5 4 3 2

Cataloging in Publication Data is on file with the Library of Congress

ISBN 978-1-60442-534-5

Discounts are available for books ordered in bulk. Special consideration is givento state bars, CLE programs, and other bar-related organizations. Inquire at BookPublishing, ABA Publishing, American Bar Association, 321 N. Clark Street, Chicago, IL 60610.

www.ababooks.org

CONTENTS

ACKNOWLEDGMENTS

Many legal practitioners contributed to this book by making suggestions for content and by recounting stories from their own experiences. They were particularly helpful in offering concrete examples to illustrate how some of the tips suggested in this book can be used in various situations involving the practice of law.

The contributors included state and federal trial and appellate court judges, civil and criminal trial lawyers, an assistant U.S. attorney, a public defender, and several public school teachers who were former practicing lawyers. Some of the contributors prefer to remain anonymous. Others have given me permission to identify them. They include the following: Ellen Cohen, assistant U.S. attorney for the Southern District of Florida; Judge Robert M. Gross of the Fourth District Court of Appeal in Florida; Carey Haughwout, public defender in the Fifteenth Judicial Circuit of Florida; and F. Gregory Barnhart, a civil trial lawyer. I am truly indebted to all these fine practitioners who gave so willingly of their time and expertise.

I must also thank attorneys Sarina Glazer and Michael S. Harley. They read the manuscript and made suggestions that were particularly valuable from their perspectives as lawyers who have also worked in schools.

David A. Sousa
Palm Beach, Florida

ABOUT THE AUTHOR

David A. Sousa, Ed.D., is an international education consultant and author of seven best-selling books (Corwin Press) on how educators and parents can translate current brain research into strategies to improve learning. He has conducted workshops in hundreds of school districts to more than 100,000 educators on brain research and science education at the pre-K to 12th grade and university levels. He has made presentations at national conventions of education organizations and to regional and local school districts across the United States, Canada, Europe, Australia, and Asia. In recent years, he has become interested in how brain research can be applied to other professions, such as law.

Dr. Sousa has a bachelor's degree in chemistry from Massachusetts State College at Bridgewater, a master of arts in teaching degree in science from Harvard University, and a doctorate in education from Rutgers University. He has taught high school science, been a school superintendent, and served as an adjunct professor of education at Seton Hall University and as a visiting lecturer at Rutgers University.

He has received awards from professional associations, school districts, and education foundations for his commitment to research, staff development, and science education. He recently received the Distinguished Alumni Award and an honorary doctorate in education from Massachusetts State College at Bridgewater. Dr. Sousa has been interviewed by Matt Lauer on the NBC *Today Show* and by National Public Radio about his work with schools using brain research.

INTRODUCTION

I not only use all the brains that I have, but all that I can borrow.

—Woodrow Wilson

Are you in any way involved in the study and practice of law? Do you want to ensure that you have the knowledge and skills necessary to be the most effective in what you do? And do you want to understand recent studies of the brain that offer information, strategies, and insights to make you more successful as a student, an advocate, a colleague, and a professional? If you answered yes to any of these questions, this book is for you.

I am not a lawyer nor have I had any formal training in legal studies. I am a lifelong science educator who, in more than 25 years, has specialized in applying the results of scientific research to education practice. In recent years, discoveries in neuroscience and cognitive psychology have revealed more and more about how the human brain learns. I have written seven best-selling books and numerous articles suggesting ways that educators can translate this exciting new brain research into their practice in schools and classrooms. However, this knowledge is not just for professional educators. It is of immense value to anyone who plays the role of a teacher and who presents information to others so that they understand and remember it. Of course, some research results just reaffirm the value of learning strategies that have been around for a long time. An important element that the research adds, however, is why the strategy works, and when we know the why, we can apply the strategy so much more masterfully.

Several practicing and retired lawyers have participated in some of the many workshops I conduct for educators in North America. Every one of them has suggested that the information I presented to professional educators would be valuable to many members of the legal profession as well. Trial lawyers in particular, they said, would benefit because they so often step into the role of teacher when presenting to a judge and jury. Judges, too, will benefit because they often have to translate complex legal nuances and technicalities into instructions that jurors of different educational backgrounds can understand. As a result of the comments made by my workshop participants, the idea for this book was born.

Lawyers as Teachers

Lawyers and judges are like teachers in one very important aspect: They often try to change someone's brain. That may sound dramatic, but that is exactly what happens when the human brain learns and remembers information—it is changed for a long time, perhaps forever. Learning changes people's brains because new connections must be made among their brain cells to store that newly acquired information. Whether it is with a client, arbitrator, colleague, judge, or jury, lawyers are usually arguing a point, explaining a rule, or defending a position in an effort to teach or convince the listener. Consequently, the more lawyers know about how the brain works, the more likely they are to be successful at helping people to learn and remember.

> *Lawyers and judges are like teachers in one very important aspect: They often try to change people's brains.*

During the last two decades, research in the neurosciences has revealed new understandings about how the brain grows, develops, and learns. Regardless of their profession, people who find themselves in teaching roles need to be aware of the new research as it applies to their practice. The most significant characteristic of a profession is that its members continue to add to their knowledge base those discoveries and insights that can allow them to be more effective with the clients they serve.

Yet law schools have not typically viewed lawyers in their role as teachers. Law school graduates have told me that considerable time is spent during legal training on understanding the law that will be applied in trials and appellate arguments—in other words, how to prepare for a hearing or trial. Some law schools offer optional courses in speech preparation. But little attention is paid to developing those understandings

> *Today, more than ever, the medium is more important than the message.*

and skills that can turn law school graduates into effective instructors and advocates. Most of the lawyers I have talked with told me that they had to learn teaching skills on the job, and they remarked about how much more effective they would have been in their early trials if they had learned those skills before facing a judge and jury.

The Tech Generation

Possessing up-to-date teaching skills is particularly important now because younger colleagues, judges, and jurors have a considerably different view of the modern world than those of us who have been around for a while. The so-called Generation X has been brought up in a multimedia environment. From early childhood, these individuals have played computer games, arcade games, and electronic games—devices that are interactive and involve rapidly changing input. The "Gen Xers" have filled their minds at will with large doses of fantasy through their games and videos, and they have communicated with the world through the Internet. E-mail has replaced much of their face-to-face communications. As a result, neuroscientists say that children and young adults who have grown up in this age of digital electronics have become acclimated to novelty. This acclimation is not the result of any changes in the brain's physical structure.

For many thousands of years, the brain has been interested in novelty, mainly because it is the new and unusual events in our environment that could pose a threat to our survival and thus capture our attention. But in the twenty-first century, the glut and persistence of media images and sounds that surround today's youth have greatly heightened the brain's sensitivity to, and preoccupation with, novel events. Today, more than ever, the medium is more important than the message.

The Gen Xers also watch movies and television programs that contain graphic violence, validate an anything-goes lifestyle, and defend disrespect for authority. Furthermore, members of this generation want to control their sources of information and to get that information rapidly. They have little patience with slower media (e.g., newspapers and lectures). They are more cynical toward government, more questioning about the established rules of conduct, and more apathetic toward their responsibilities as citizens.

Current trends in jury reform are also changing the nature of juries. One trend is to expand the pool of potential jurors. For many years, prospective jurors were drawn from the lists of registered voters. The idea was that these registrants were more apt to accept jury service as one of

> *Lawyers and judges will need new approaches to communicate with juries composed of members who are acclimated to novelty.*

the responsibilities of citizenship. Efforts to expand this pool have now led many jurisdictions to include licensed drivers and utility bill payers, raising the probability that more people will be doing their jury duty begrudgingly.

Another trend is to get jurors more involved during trial. Many jurisdictions now allow jurors to take notes while sitting in the jury box. In 2004, the Colorado courts allowed jurors in criminal cases to send written questions to the judge during the trial, a procedure that had been used in the state for five years in civil cases. For members of the legal profession, the current generation's desire for novelty will have significant implications when these individuals are called to serve on a jury.

Impact on Juries

Juries are already enough of a mystery that an entire industry of jury consultants has emerged to give advice on the best ways to select jurors and argue a case. These consultants are not always right. Lawyers and judges will need new approaches to communicate with juries composed of members who are acclimated to novelty. Sonya Hamlin, author of *What Makes Juries Listen Today*, notes that this generation has difficulty focusing on the testimony of expert witnesses, which is often boring, fact-filled, sequential, and tedious. These jurors, she contends, are accustomed to getting large doses of unreality and fantasy at the click of a mouse or a remote. The grim experiences of the real world as well as the formal structure and nonvisual nature of courtroom trials may not be sufficient to maintain their interest. The mind-set of younger jurors will be quite different from older jurors' who may never have used e-mail or played electronic games, dislike 10-second video clips, abhor violence, believe strongly in the responsibilities of citizenship, and are comfortable listening to lengthy verbal presentations.

Just what parts of the typical trial scenario are the novelty-acclimated generation likely to find wearisome? Here are some good possibilities:

- Lengthy opening statements
- Long, tedious, highly technical expert testimony
- Continuous reexplanation of evidence already presented
- Repetition of testimony
- Lengthy closing statements without graphics of talking points
- Overuse of legal jargon

The implications of how lawyers and judges communicate with modern juries need to be studied carefully. Nonetheless, one can argue that (1) judges should give instructions to juries that include simple examples of legal principles and that are accompanied by visual representations, (2) the lawyers' opening statements should be brief and avoid in-depth analysis of individuals and facts, (3) attention should be paid to maintaining the jurors' interest, and (4) the trial should be streamlined to move at the pace of the modern multimedia world. Closing statements, which are usually longer, should include graphics when their use will clarify complex issues for both judges and jurors.

Why This Book Can Help

The aim of this book is to help anyone who has to teach important information about the law. I report on research (from neuroscience as well as the behavioral and cognitive sciences) that is sufficiently reliable that it can inform instructional practice. At the same time, I provide examples of how these applications can be used in law-related settings. Because many readers will be unfamiliar with neuroscience, I avoid writing in an academic style. My goal is not to make neuroscientists out of lawyers. Rather it is to provide enough knowledge and understanding about what we are learning in brain science so that lawyers can be more effective in carrying out their professional responsibilities.

Questions This Book Will Answer

This book will help answer such questions as the following:

- What can this research tell me about how my own brain learns?
- How can I use the scientific research on how the brain learns to improve my work and my workplace?
- What trial strategies are likely to be effective with listeners who have grown up in a fast-paced multimedia society?
- At what point during my presentations are people most likely to remember what I said?
- What techniques can I use to help listeners understand and remember more of what I am presenting?
- Why are learning styles so important and what can I do about them?
- How do I help my listeners find meaning in the information I am presenting so that they are more likely to remember it?
- What length of presentation is most effective?
- What is the maximum number of items I should include in my presentation at any one time?
- How do I deal with the listeners' emotions that may emerge during my presentations?

- Which type of graphic organizer is most appropriate in a given situation?
- What type of model framework will help me formulate a successful scope and sequence for my presentation?
- What questions should I be asking myself while designing presentations so that they will be effective?

Who Should Use This Book?

This book will be useful to law professionals (i.e., practicing lawyers, judges, and paraprofessionals who interact with clients) because it presents a research-based rationale for why and when certain instructional strategies should be considered. It focuses on the brain as the organ of thinking and learning, and takes the approach that the more lawyers, judges, and paraprofessionals know about how the brain learns, the more instructional options that become available.

> *This book will be useful to lawyers, judges, paraprofessionals, and law school instructors.*

Increasing these options also increases the likelihood that listeners and observers will pay attention and learn. I have intentionally avoided getting into detailed and complex scientific explanations of the discoveries that neuroscientists have made. My intent is to present just enough science to help the average reader understand the research and the rationale for any suggestions I offer.

Law school professors will find merit in the research and applications presented here. The instructional suggestions may improve their own teaching as well as become part of the information and strategies they pass on to their students who are prospective lawyers.

A valuable aspect of this book is that it includes specific suggestions of how this research translates into effective office and courtroom techniques that improve the practice of law. The suggestions are presented as numbered tips (Tip 1.1, etc.). Many of the examples come from my interviews with practicing lawyers and judges. Readers are invited to critically review my suggestions and rationale to determine whether they have value for their work. Although this book does not specifically address presentations designed to sell a law firm to prospective clients, some of the strategies suggested here can be easily modified for that purpose.

Chapter Content

In the ensuing chapters, we will examine how new revelations from neuroscience can help those of you in the legal profession become more effective in your work.

Chapter 1, Understanding Your Brain, discusses ways in which you can keep your own brain healthy and learn about how your brain views and interprets the world. Part of this interpretation is formed by preferences you have for sensory input and whether more of your left or right hemisphere of the brain is used during complex thinking. Two self-assessments are included to help you determine these preferences. Results from the assessments give you insights into how you learn and, consequently, how you present information to others—in other words, how you teach. Also included is a self-assessment designed to measure personality traits associated with creativity. Analyzing these results will raise your awareness about how well you stand up for what is right, how willing you are to try new things, and whether you motivate others.

Chapter 2, Using Your Brain in the Workplace, looks at how to apply brain science to improving your effectiveness in your workplace. It discusses some of the research on leaders' habits of mind as opposed to managers' habits, and suggests some strategies for using your brain power to enhance the productivity and positive climate of the workplace.

Chapter 3, Applying Brain Research to Your Practice, moves the applications of brain research from the office where you prepare your work to the arena where you practice law. That arena may be the conference room where you meet with clients, or it may be the courtroom where you argue your case as a trial lawyer or render decisions as a judge. For law professors, it may be the classrooms where you teach.

Chapter 4, Putting It All Together, combines important information from the previous chapters into a suggested design for planning your presentations. It offers a list of questions to ask yourself as you put your presentation together. The design and the questions provide a framework that allows you to incorporate the scientific discoveries about how the brain works into your daily practice of law.

The appendix, Basic Brain Facts, contains more technical information for readers who want to learn a bit more about brain structures and functions.

Main thoughts are highlighted in shadow boxes throughout the book. At the end of each chapter, you will find the Key Points to Ponder, an organizing tool to help you remember important ideas, strategies, and resources you may wish to consider later. A glossary is included to define the scientific terms used in the book. In the Recommended Reading section, I include some of the sources that I used in writing the text, and I suggest some books and articles that expand on many of the major topics presented here.

Nearly everyone working in the legal profession has to present information to someone at sometime—whether it be to clients, jurors, judges, colleagues, or students. The more you know about how the brain attends, processes, and learns, the more effective your design and delivery of that presentation will be. My hope is that this book will provide you with some new information, strategies, and insights that will make you more successful as an advocate, a colleague, and a professional.

Note: This book does not deal with how research in neuroscience may eventually affect some basic constructs in law, such as competency, free will, or the causes of violent behavior, and whether such information should be introduced in testimony. For more information on this controversial area, contact the Dana Foundation at www.dana.org.

CHAPTER 1

Understanding Your Brain

Only as you do know yourself can your brain serve you as a sharp and efficient tool. Know your own failings, passions, and prejudices so you can separate them from what you see.

—Bernard Baruch

Have you ever stopped to think about how your brain gets you through your workday? Apart from its obvious and vital role in coordinating movement and internal body functions, the brain also has to simultaneously process an enormous amount of external data that are bombarding your senses every second while you are awake. As the brain does its processing, it continually sends summaries of what is going on to your consciousness:

    . . . Ouch, the shower water is too hot!
    . . . Smells like the coffee is ready.
    . . . I hear the phone ringing; do you want to answer it?
    . . . I see the clock reads 7:47 already; you're late for work.
    . . . I can hear the rain; bring an umbrella.

The brain's phenomenal ability to handle all this information and to make continuous decisions, both consciously and subconsciously, has been the subject of intense scientific interest in recent years. Especially since the 1990's "Decade of the Brain," researchers have poked, probed, and viewed the living brain from all angles, using highly sophisticated imaging techniques. As a result, they have made fascinating discoveries about how the brain works. Of particular interest to cognitive scientists has been how the brain develops and adapts to its environment from birth through adulthood. During that growth period, experiences are shaping each brain and designing the unique cellular architecture that will influence how it handles future experiences in school, work, and other places. Because no two people grow up with identical sets of experiences, no two people see and interact with their world in exactly the same way. People are different from each other in many ways—not just physically, but mentally as well.

In this chapter, we look first at brain health, that is, we review the kinds of things you should be doing, eating, and drinking to keep your brain in topnotch condition. Then we examine the different ways in which people process and interpret sensory data, and how this affects the way they learn. We also discuss the fascinating topic of left-brain, right-brain preferences, otherwise known as hemisphericity. Despite the criticism this work received when it was overhyped during the 1980s, the concept still provides scientifically valid and useful information that can help us understand how we view and react to our world. Finally, we look at the astonishing notion that creativity is a separate ability from intelligence, and we explore some common characteristics of creative people.

TIP 1.1: Keep Your Brain Nourished

Keep your brain well nourished throughout the day. Brain cells (like all our body cells) need plenty of oxygen, glucose, water and other nutrients to function effectively. Although the brain represents about 2 percent of your body weight, it consumes 20 percent of your calories. What you eat and drink can greatly affect your motivation, mood, and mental performance.

What Your Brain Needs to Stay Sharp

Start with Oxygen and Glucose. Brain cells consume oxygen and glucose (a form of sugar) for fuel. The more challenging the brain's task, the more fuel it consumes. Take steps to ensure that you have adequate amounts of these fuels present in the brain for optimum functioning, especially if you have a tough mental task ahead. Low amounts of oxygen and glucose in the blood can produce lethargy and sleepiness, and dampen mental performance. So, when possible, find ways to keep the blood well oxygenated. Take the stairs instead of the elevator. Park your car farther from the building entrance so you have a greater distance to walk. These little inconveniences pump up your metabolism and increase the amount of much-needed oxygen in your blood. When working on a particularly arduous task, get up from your desk and walk around about every 30 minutes. Take several deep breaths periodically to increase your oxygen levels and alertness. This deep breathing works best if you breathe in through your nose and out through your mouth.

Many people do not eat a breakfast that contains sufficient glucose to maintain optimum blood-sugar levels. Eating a moderate portion of food containing glucose (fruits and cereals are excellent sources) along with moderate exercise to increase oxygen levels can boost the performance and accuracy of working memory, attention, and motor function. Stay away from foods that contain high fructose corn syrup as the main sweetener. They just add to your waistline without providing the glucose your brain cells

> *Many people do not eat a breakfast with sufficient glucose nor drink enough water during the day for healthy brain function.*

need for fuel. Doughnuts and other pastries usually contain dextrose or sucrose. These are large sugar molecules that are not readily converted to energy and are more likely to be stored, thereby adding weight.

Food throughout Your Day. For a challenging early morning PowerPoint® presentation, crank up the glucose with oatmeal and brown sugar. They provide a quick shot of glucose for the brain. If you hate oatmeal, try a banana or a plain bagel. The lack of fat in a bagel allows the body to turn it into glucose fast. If you have an unexpected meeting that demands brain power, eat some raisins—a rich source of boron. Researchers at the U.S. Department of Agriculture have found that boosting the amount of boron in the body provides an immediate increase (about 10 percent) in attention and memory recall. Apples and nuts are also rich in boron.

Having a power lunch or working overtime? Try an egg salad sandwich and milk. Studies at the University of North Carolina have shown that choline (eggs and milk are rich sources) promotes the release of acetylcholine—a neurotransmitter that helps your brain store and retrieve information. Choline pills can also be taken as a supplement.

Remember Water. Water, also essential for healthy brain activity, is required to move signals through the brain cells. Low concentrations of water diminish the rate and efficiency of these signals. Moreover, water keeps the lungs sufficiently moist to allow for the efficient transfer of oxygen into the bloodstream. Make sure that you and your staff drink plenty of water. How much water is enough? The long-standing recommendation that everyone should drink eight 8-ounce glasses of water a day is no longer the standard. The current recommended amount is one 8-ounce glass of water a day for each 25 pounds of body weight. Thus, a 150-pound person needs about six glasses per day (150/25 = 6). Keep in mind, however, that many other liquid drinks, such as soda and iced tea, count toward this total. And a word of caution: Drinking too much water can deplete the body of vital minerals, such as sodium, potassium, and calcium (required for maintaining heart, brain, and muscle function), not to mention require more frequent trips to the bathroom.

Check in advance if you can bring bottled water to the courtroom. Both air-conditioning and heating greatly reduce the humidity in the courtroom, leading to slow but consistent dehydration. As water evaporates from your body, your blood flow becomes sluggish and brain signals move slower. If water is not allowed in the courtroom, request frequent breaks to replenish this vital body fluid and to keep you alert.

Other Nutrients. Intellectual performance requires certain fats in your diet, known as omega-3 fatty acids, which are commonly found in fish. The omega-3s are used to make the outer membrane of brain cells through which all nerve signals must pass (see the appendix). Furthermore, as learning and memory create new connections between nerve cells, new membranes must be formed to protect them. Thus, brain cell membranes need a continuous supply of fatty acids. Good sources of omega-3s are salmon, tuna, sardine, mackerel, and herring. For vegetarians, use flaxseed oil. Omega-3s are also available in capsule form at nutrition stores.

B vitamins (including B1, B5, B6, and B12) and folic acid are essential for boosting mood, alertness, and memory as well as improving the brain's resistance to stress. They are important for maintaining your supply of neurotransmitters—those chemicals that move signals from one brain cell to another. Many people, unfortunately, do not have a sufficient amount of B vitamins in their diet. Foods rich in B vitamins and folic acid are whole-grain breads and rice, fish, meat, poultry, fruits, vegetables, eggs, and milk and other dairy products.

Minerals play a vital role in nerve function by moderating signals that move through and between brain cells. Three important minerals are magnesium (found in whole grains, nuts, and green vegetables), potassium (found in bananas, cantaloupe, grapefruit, honeydew, potatoes, meat, and fish), and calcium (found in milk and dairy products, such as cheese and yogurt).

Avoid the herbal supplements, such a ginkgo biloba, that claim to stimulate the brain. No credible scientific studies to date have shown that these supplements actually improve brain functions or memory. If you really want to improve your memory, see the strategies suggested later in this chapter.

Antioxidants. Finally, don't forget the antioxidants. Although cells rely on oxygen for fuel, certain highly reactive forms of oxygen can actually damage brain cells (as well as other body cells). These highly reactive molecules, called free radicals, damage cells faster than they can be repaired. Over time, this kind of radical attack can result in diminished brain function. To offset this attack, the brain needs a constant supply of antioxidants to keep the free radicals under control. This is especially true for older adults because the amount of natural antioxidants in our body decreases as we age. The antioxidant supply can come from diet or through supplements. Effective antioxidants include vitamin C, vitamin E, and coenzyme Q10, all available as supplements. Beware, however, of high-dose supplements of vitamin E.

The recommended daily intake for this vitamin is 22.5 international units (IU) per day. The most common dosage of over-the-counter E supplements is 400 IU. A research study conducted in 2004 at the Johns Hopkins School of Medicine indicated that high doses of vitamin E (i.e., more than 150 IU per day) may actually increase the risk of "all-cause" death. Because the average adult gets only about 10 to 15 IU from diet, eat more natural sources of vitamin E, such a green leafy vegetables, nuts, and vegetable oils. Otherwise, take a typical multivitamin tablet, most of which contain 30 to 45 IU of vitamin E.

Stay in good physical and mental condition. It's a gift you give yourself. You'll work better if you feel better. Table 1.1 summarizes the essential ingredients for feeding and maintaining a healthy brain.

Understanding Our World

One of the brain's most important functions is to collect, process, and interpret information from the environment so that we can learn how to survive. While performing this vital task, the brain dedicates specific regions in each of its hemispheres to process certain kinds of information. For example, in most people, spoken language is processed in two specialized regions in the left hemisphere and visual information is processed across the rear of the brain.

As we interact with our environment and learn, we begin to develop preferences in how we collect and process new information and skills. These preferences develop early in life and result from genetic

Component	Function	Sources
TABLE 1.1 ESSENTIALS FOR A HEALTHY BRAIN		
Oxygen	Necessary fuel for cell metabolism	Exercise increases amount of oxygen in blood
Glucose	Necessary fuel for cell metabolism	Fruits, cereals, and breads
Water	Moves brain signals efficiently; moistens lungs for increased oxygen intake	Water, fruits, other beverages
Omega-3 fatty acids	Build brain cell membranes	Fish, such as salmon, tuna, sardine, mackerel, and herring; also flaxseed oil.
B vitamins (B1, B5, B6, B12, and folic acid)	For production of neurotransmitters; to enhance mood, memory, and alertness; protect against stress	Whole-grain breads and rice, fish, meat, poultry, fruits, eggs, vegetables, milk and dairy products
Minerals (magnesium, potassium, calcium, and boron)	Moderate signals moving through and between brain cells	Whole grains, nuts, vegetables, bananas, cantaloupe, grapefruit, honeydew, potatoes, meat, fish, and raisins
Antioxidants	Prevent free radicals from damaging brain cells	Vitamin C, vitamin E, and coenzyme Q10

predispositions and environmental influences, and they become particularly evident during prolonged and complex learning tasks. Among the different types of learning preferences, two are of particular interest because they can have such a powerful effect on how we view the world. The first relates to favoring one or more of our senses over the others, and is known as sensory preference. The second describes the tendency to use one hemisphere more than the other when processing complex material, which is known as hemispheric preference. Although scientists have rightly criticized the extreme interpretations that some people have made about both of these preferences, many still acknowledge that some valid implications can be drawn.

TIP 1.2: Know Your Own Sensory Preference(s)

We use all five senses to collect information from our environment, but over time they do not contribute equally to our knowledge base. As adults, sight, hearing, and touch regularly contribute more new knowledge than do taste and smell. We learn something new each day just by reading the newspaper or watching television. But, unless you work in a perfume factory or gourmet kitchen, you do not encounter a new smell or taste very often.

Most of us do not even use sight, hearing, and touch equally during learning. Just as we develop a left- or right-handed preference, we also develop preferences for certain senses as we process information. For example, some people have a preference for collecting more visual information during learning. They are called visually preferred learners. Others who use hearing as the preferred sense are known as auditorily preferred learners. Still others who prefer touch or whole-body involvement in their learn-

> *Knowing your own sensory and hemispheric preferences can give you insight into how you view the world.*

ing are called kinesthetically preferred learners. Sensory preferences are just that—preferences. After all, right-handed people still use their left hand to accomplish many tasks. Nonetheless, these sensory preferences are an important component of an individual's learning style, because they influence how that person interacts with the environment and teaches others. Teaching others is a part of lawyering, so let's determine your sensory preferences with the following activity.

Determining Your Sensory Preferences

The following assessment will help you determine your sensory preference(s). It is designed for adults and is one of many that are available. Remember that sensory preferences are usually evident only during prolonged and complex learning tasks.

Directions. For each item, circle "A" if you agree that the statement describes you most of the time. Circle "D" if you disagree that the statement describes you most of the time. Move quickly through the questions. Your first response is usually the more accurate one.

1. I prefer reading a story rather than listening to someone tell it.   A   D

2. I would rather watch television than listen to the radio.   A   D

3. I remember faces better than names.   A   D

4. I like my office to have lots of pictures around the room.   A   D

5. The appearance of my handwriting is important to me.   A   D

6. I think more often in pictures.   A   D

7. I am distracted by visual disorder or movement.   A   D

8. I have difficulty remembering directions that were told to me.   A   D

9. I would rather watch athletic events than participate in them.   A   D

10. I tend to organize my thoughts by writing them down.   A   D

11. My facial expression is a good indicator of my emotions.   A   D

12. I tend to remember names better than faces.   A   D

13. I would enjoy taking part in dramatic events like plays.   A   D

14. I tend to subvocalize and think in sounds.   A   D

15. I am easily distracted by sounds.   A   D

16. I easily forget what I read unless I talk about it.   A   D

17. I would rather listen to the radio than watch television.   A   D

18. My handwriting is not very good.   A   D

19. When faced with a problem, I tend to talk it through.   A   D

20. I express my emotions verbally.   A   D

21. I would rather be in a group discussion than read about a topic.   A   D

22. I prefer talking on the phone rather than writing a letter to someone.	A	D
23. I would rather participate in athletic events than watch them.	A	D
24. I prefer going to museums where I can touch the exhibits.	A	D
25. My handwriting deteriorates when the space becomes smaller.	A	D
26. My mental pictures are usually accompanied by movement.	A	D
27. I like being outdoors and doing things like biking, camping, swimming, hiking, etc.	A	D
28. I remember best what was done rather than what was seen or talked about.	A	D
29. When faced with a problem, I often select the solution involving the greatest activity.	A	D
30. I like to make models or other hand-crafted items.	A	D
31. I would rather do experiments than read about them.	A	D
32. My body language is a good indicator of my emotions.	A	D
33. I have difficulty remembering verbal directions if I have not done the activity before.	A	D

Interpreting Your Score. Total the following responses to determine your visual, auditory, and tactile/kinesthetic scores.

Total the number of "A" responses in items 1–11: _____
This is your visual score.
Total the number of "A" responses in items 12–22: _____
This is your auditory score.
Total the number of "A" responses in items 23–33: _____
This is your tactile/kinesthetic score.

If one of your scores is five or more points higher than your scores for the other two areas, this sense is most probably your preference during a protracted and complex learning situation.

If one of your scores is five or more points lower than your scores for the other two areas, this sense is not likely to be your preference in a protracted learning situation.

If your scores are similar across all three areas, you can learn things in almost any way they are presented.

Reflections

- What was your preferred sense? Were you surprised?

- How does this preference show up when you are presenting information to others?

TIP 1.3: Know Whether You Are Left-Brained or Right-Brained

At first look, this section might seem like something from 1980s pop culture because much light was made in the media about the peculiarities of left-brained and right-brained people. Unfortunately, popular and wildly inaccurate interpretations overwhelmed the beneficial aspects relating to the discovery in the 1960s that the two halves of the human brain had areas of specialization. Let's put the hype aside. Here we discuss in nontechnical terms what science discovered and how this knowledge gives us greater insight into ways our brain's processing preferences influence our thinking and personality.

Hemispheric Preference

More evidence is accumulating that the brain may be a set of modular units that carry out specific tasks. According to this modular model, the brain is a collection of units that supports the mind's information-processing requirements, and not a singular unit whose every part is capable of any function. After nearly 40 years of case studies and, more recently, brain scans, researchers have observed considerable consistency in the different ways the two halves of the brain store and process information. This cerebral specialization is also called hemisphericity. Researchers now explain the differences in the way the two hemispheres process information as follows.

Left Hemisphere. The left side appears to be the logical hem   `ore.
It monitors the areas for speech, is analytical, and evaluates fact`
rial in a rational way. It understands the literal interpretatior
and detects time units and sequence. It also recognizes wc
and numbers written as words.

Right Hemisphere. The right brain responds like the i`
sphere. It gathers information more from images than fr

10

probes for patterns. It interprets speech through context—body language, emotional content, and tone of voice—rather than through literal meanings. It specializes in spatial perceptions and is the area in which visual creativity may originate. It also recognizes places, faces, and objects. Table 1.2 specifies these and other functions that the hemispheres seem to perform as they deal with vast amounts of new and past information that must be interpreted and assessed every second.

Specialization Does Not Mean Exclusivity. The research data support the notion that each hemisphere has its own set of functions in information processing and thinking. These functions, however, are seldom exclusive to only one hemisphere, and in even some simple tasks, it is possible for both hemispheres to be involved. In the average individual, the results of the separate processing are exchanged with the opposite hemisphere. There is harmony in the goals of each, and they complement one another in almost all activities. Thus, the individual benefits from the integration of the processing done by both hemispheres and is afforded greater comprehension of whatever situation started the processing.

> *Most people have a preferred hemisphere. This preference affects their personality, abilities, and learning style.*

Hemispheric Preference: A Question of Learning (and Presenting) Style. Continuing studies of the brain using imaging and other techniques show that most people often rely more on one hemisphere during complex processing, and that this preference affects personality, abilities, and learning style. The preference runs the gamut from neutral (no preference) to strongly left- or right-hemisphere preferred. Those who are left-hemisphere preferred tend to be more verbal, analytical, and able to solve sequential problems. Right-hemisphere-preferred individuals paint and draw well, are good at mathematics and solving open-ended problems, and deal with the visual world more easily than with the verbal.

Once again, the preference for either hemisphere does not mean that we do not use both hemispheres. In doing a simple task, we use the brain region in the hemisphere that will accomplish the task more efficiently. When we are faced with a task that is more complex, however, the preferred hemisphere will often take the lead, although the nonpreferred hemisphere will almost certainly get involved as well.

Examples of Preference. Suppose you are right-handed. A pencil is on the table just next to your left hand, and someone asks you to pass

Left-Hemisphere Functions	Right-Hemisphere Functions
TABLE 1.2 *FUNCTIONS OF THE LEFT AND RIGHT BRAIN HEMISPHERES*	
Connected to right side of body	Connected to left side of body
Processes input in a sequential and analytical manner	Processes input more holistically and abstractly
Time sensitive	Space sensitive
Generates spoken language	Interprets language through gestures, facial movements, emotions, and body language
Does invariable and arithmetic operations	Does relational and mathematical operations
Specializes in recognizing words and numbers (as words)	Specializes in recognizing faces, places, objects, and music
Active in constructing false memories	More truthful in recall
Seeks explanations for why events occur	Puts events in spatial patterns
Better at arousing attention to deal with outside stimuli	Better at internal processing

the pencil. Because this is a simple task, you will pick up the pencil with your left hand in a smooth motion and pass it. You are not likely to stretch your right hand across your body or twist your torso to hand it over. However, if the person asks you to throw the pencil, you will probably use your right hand because this task is more difficult and requires accuracy.

During learning, both hemispheres are engaged, processing the information or skill according to their specializations and exchanging the results with the opposite hemisphere through a connecting nerve cable called the corpus callosum (see the appendix). So if someone were to toss a pencil to you, your likelihood of successfully catching it increases greatly if you use both hands, not just your right (dominant) hand.

Knowing the difference between how the left and right hemispheres process information explains why we succeed with some tasks but not with others, especially when we are trying to do them simultaneously. For instance, most of us can carry on a conversation (primarily left-hemisphere activity) while cooking a familiar meal (primarily right-hemisphere activity). In this example, each task is largely (but not exclusively) controlled by different hemispheres. But trying to carry on a conversation on the telephone while talking to someone in the room at the same time is difficult because these are functions of the same (left) hemisphere that can interfere with each other.

Implications of Preference for Your Presentations. Hemispheric preference is another component of your learning style. We noted earlier that because you will tend to present information the same way you learn it, you need to know as much about your learning style as possible. Besides telling you something about yourself, this knowledge helps you understand that your listeners can have different styles.

Testing Your Hemispheric Preference

There are several instruments available to assess hemispheric preference. The one below takes just a few minutes and will give you an indication of your preference. The results are not conclusive, so if this is an area of particular interest, you may wish to seek out additional instruments to collect more data before reaching any firm conclusion about your hemispheric preference.

Directions. From each pair below, circle A or B corresponding to the sentence that best describes you. Do not spend too much time with any one question. Your first response is usually the most accurate. Answer all questions. There are no right or wrong answers.

1. A. I prefer to find my own way of doing a new task.
   B. I prefer to be told the best way to do a new task.

2. A. I have to make my own plans.
   B. I can follow anyone's plans.

3. A. I am a very flexible and occasionally unpredictable person.
   B. I am a very stable and consistent person.

4. A. I keep everything in a particular place.
   B. Where I keep things depends on what I am doing.

5. A.   I spread my work evenly over the time I have.
    B.   I prefer to do my work at the last minute.

6. A.   I know I am right because I have good reasons.
    B.   I know when I am right, even without reasons.

7. A.   I need a lot of variety and change in my life.
    B.   I need a well-planned and orderly life.

8. A.   I sometimes have too many ideas in a new situation.
    B.   I sometimes don't have any ideas in a new situation.

9. A.   I do easy things first and the important things last.
    B.   I do the important things first and the easy things last.

10. A.   I choose what I know is right when making a hard decision.
    B.   I choose what I feel is right when making a hard decision.

11. A.   I plan my time for doing my work.
    B.   I don't think about the time when I work.

12. A.   I usually have good self-discipline.
    B.   I usually act on my feelings.

13. A.   Other people don't understand how I organize things.
    B.   Other people think I organize things well.

14. A.   I agree with new ideas before other people do.
    B.   I question new ideas more than other people do.

15. A.   I tend to think more in pictures.
    B.   I tend to think more in words.

16. A.   I try to find the one best way to solve a problem.
    B.   I try to find different ways to solve a problem.

17. A.   I can usually analyze what is going to happen next.
    B.   I can usually sense what is going to happen next.

18. A.   I am not very imaginative in my work.
    B.   I use my imagination in nearly everything I do.

19. A.   I begin many jobs that I never finish.
    B.   I finish a job before starting a new one.

20. A.   I look for new ways to do old jobs.
    B.   When one way works well, I don't change it.

21. A.   It is fun to take risks.
    B.   I have fun without taking risks.

Interpreting Your Score. Count the number of A and B responses to the following questions to determine your hemispheric preference.

Count the number of "A" responses to   A: _____
questions 1, 3, 7, 8, 9, 13, 14, 15, 19, 20, and 21.
Place that number on the line to the right.

Count the number of "B" responses to   B: _____
the remaining questions. Place that number
on the line to the right.

Total the "A" and "B" responses.   Total: _____

The total indicates your hemispheric preference according to the following scale:

0–5: Strong left hemisphere preference

6–8: Moderate left hemisphere preference

9–12: Bilateral hemisphere balance (little or no preference)

13–15: Moderate right hemisphere preference

16–21: Strong right hemisphere preference

Reflections

- Did your score surprise you? Why or why not?

- What does your score tell you about your presentations?

TIP 1.4: Assess Your Creative Traits

The front part of the brain (behind the forehead) is the executive (also called rational) system of the brain and is the most likely place where creative thought occurs. When people are creative by thinking outside the box, they usually get a feeling of enjoyment and pride in what they have accomplished. Accordingly, the emotional areas buried deeper in the brain also contribute to fostering creative behaviors. The interaction of the emotional and rational systems can generate the intrinsic motivation that seems so important for creative people to continue to produce.

15

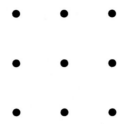

Figure 1.1 Without lifting the pencil, connect all nine dots with just four straight lines. Do not retrace over a line or go through a dot more than once.

Directions. Look at figure 1.1. Follow the directions and connect all nine dots with just four straight lines. Do not lift the pencil off the paper and do not retrace a line or go through a dot more than once. If you are having difficulty solving this puzzle, ask yourself what limitations you may be inadvertently setting up. The solution requires you to literally think outside the box. (If you get stuck, the answer is located at the end of the appendix.)

Is Creativity Different from Intelligence?

Recent studies on the brain have revealed some fascinating insights into how the brain responds when solving different types of problems. In one such study, Slovenian researcher Norbert Jausovec tested about 50 young adults for intelligence by having them use convergent thinking to solve a series of logical and sequential problems. They were tested for creativity by solving open-ended problems that required divergent thinking. By measuring brain waves, the researchers discovered that the areas of the brain used to solve problems requiring intelligence were different from those used to solve problems through creativity. Apparently, the brain treats creativity and intelligence as separate abilities and recruits different areas while solving complex problems. These scientific findings confirm a reality that many of us have already observed: Smart people are not always creative, and creative people are not always smart.

> *The brain treats creativity and intelligence as separate abilities and uses different cerebral areas when solving complex problems.*

Only a few participants in Jausovec's study excelled at solving both sequential and open-ended problems. Their brain data showed that they were able to move back and forth through different cerebral

16

regions as the type of problem they were solving changed. For lack of a better term, Jausovec called them gifted.

Creativity and the Law

Most people tend to associate creativity with the arts, but it can occur in any field. To be creative, an idea must be appropriate, useful, and actionable. That's what makes it different from fantasy. Somehow, it must influence the way something gets done, either by improving a product or by opening up a new way to approach a process.

I repeat that I am not a lawyer. Nonetheless, it seems to me that creativity is essential to the practice of law. A creative lawyer finds ways to apply statutes, rules, and precedents to make different arguments for a new situation. As society evolves, rules of law that once were enacted in a past context may need to be applied differently in a contemporary context. Each new application of law gives rise to changes that represent the law as a dynamic, changing force.

> *A creative lawyer finds ways to apply statues, rules, and precedents to make different arguments for a new situation.*

To be creative, lawyers have to possess creative thinking skills, expertise, and motivation. Creative thinking skills refer to how people approach problems and solutions as well as their ability to put existing concepts together in nontraditional combinations: "What's another way to interpret the statute in this situation?" Expertise includes all that a person knows and can do in carrying out a task or job. It is difficult to be realistically creative if one does not possess all the information and skills needed to put ideas together in unexpected ways.

How a person uses expertise and creative thinking skills is often determined by motivation. There are two types of motivation: extrinsic and intrinsic. Extrinsic motivation comes from outside the person, and usually involves rewards for completing a job and punishment for not. Salary is a classic example of an extrinsic motivator. Many people work unhappily in their jobs mainly because their salary allows them to do the things they really desire. Although extrinsic motivation does not deter creativity, it rarely helps it either. True creativity is likely to come forth when the driving force is an internal desire to do something. This is intrinsic motivation. In this instance, the work itself is motivating, and the person engages in it for the challenge and the enjoyment. Salary is of less interest.

17

What makes a person creative, and more important, what makes a person creative in the workplace? There are no simple answers to these questions, but researchers tend to explain creativity in the workplace through certain habits of mind that are common to very successful innovators and leaders. A major study carried out by Jeanie Goertz found that these characteristics include the following:

- Passion for work, the ability to mix personal and professional energy and enthusiasm
- Independence, the ability to initiate and sustain autonomous thought and action
- Goal setting, the ability to select a task and complete it
- Originality, the ability to develop novel approaches in problem solving
- Flexibility, the ability to adapt to new situations and ideas
- Wide range of interests, shows interest in a variety of subjects and participates in events outside of work
- Intelligence, beyond an IQ (intelligence quotient) of 120
- Motivation, the need to achieve in all attempted activities and to self-evaluate

Although Goertz's work was done mainly with successful educational administrators, many of these characteristics were found also by researchers who studied other professions. Here is an opportunity for you to assess your own creative traits using the Goertz framework.

Assessing Your Creative Traits

Directions. Using the following scale as a guide, circle the number that best represents the extent to which each statement reflects your behavior. Move quickly through the questions. There are no right or wrong answers. When done, read the section on interpreting your score.

Scale:
1 **Never**　2 **Infrequently**　3 **Sometimes**　4 **Frequently**　5 **Always**

---

1. I enjoy going to work each day.	1	2	3	4	5
2. I have a clear vision of my goals for this organization.	1	2	3	4	5

3. I am willing to listen to unusual
   solutions offered by others. 1 2 3 4 5

4. I am curious about a lot of different
   things that can affect this organization. 1 2 3 4 5

5. I am enthusiastic about my own ideas. 1 2 3 4 5

6. I communicate my goals for this
   organization to the staff. 1 2 3 4 5

7. I look for creative ways to solve
   problems. 1 2 3 4 5

8. I analyze potential solutions for their
   advantages and disadvantages. 1 2 3 4 5

9. I am enthusiastic about my work. 1 2 3 4 5

10. I prefer to work alone. 1 2 3 4 5

11. When looking for solutions to
    problems, I prefer variety to quantity. 1 2 3 4 5

12. I am innovative in my approach to
    problem solving and decision making. 1 2 3 4 5

13. I display intellectual curiosity. 1 2 3 4 5

14. I have self-confidence. 1 2 3 4 5

15. Intellectual play is as important as
    intellectual work. 1 2 3 4 5

16. I am not comfortable with
    arbitrary rules. 1 2 3 4 5

17. I commit myself to those principles
    I believe in. 1 2 3 4 5

18. The goals of our organization are achiev-
    able within a reasonable time frame. 1 2 3 4 5

19. I take chances. 1 2 3 4 5

20. I adapt to change. 1 2 3 4 5

21. I have a wide range of interests
    outside of my job. 1 2 3 4 5

22. I encourage colleagues and staff to
    explore new ways to solve old problems. 1 2 3 4 5

23. I encourage others to understand
    my views.   1   2   3   4   5

24. I enjoy pursuing the "what if" types
    of questions.   1   2   3   4   5

25. I have a clear vision of this
    organization's mission.   1   2   3   4   5

26. I lose track of the number of hours I
    spend on my job.   1   2   3   4   5

27. I enjoy deviating from routine.   1   2   3   4   5

28. I try to give the staff as much time
    as needed to generate a variety of
    ideas for solving problems.   1   2   3   4   5

29. Listening to others is one of the most
    important parts of my job.   1   2   3   4   5

30. I can draw on my experiences outside
    my job to solve job-related problems. 1   2   3   4   5

31. I present my ideas to others
    enthusiastically.   1   2   3   4   5

32. I look at my work as play.   1   2   3   4   5

33. I prefer to make my own decisions.   1   2   3   4   5

34. I consider myself to be an effective
    role model.   1   2   3   4   5

35. Major initiatives must be consistent
    with the goals I have set for this
    organization.   1   2   3   4   5

36. I recognize that the solutions to
    some problems may have to
    wait until next year.   1   2   3   4   5

37. I tend to get input from lots of sources
    when solving a problem.   1   2   3   4   5

38. I encourage people to do more
    than they think they can.   1   2   3   4   5

39. I enjoy taking risks in my job.   1   2   3   4   5

40. I support and give credit to others
who have creative ideas.   1   2   3   4   5

41. I am persistent when it comes to
solving problems.   1   2   3   4   5

42. I am able to complete the work that is
directed toward my goals.   1   2   3   4   5

43. I do not feel like I have to make the
same decisions that my colleagues do.   1   2   3   4   5

44. When forming a committee, I want to
have a wide variety of views
represented.   1   2   3   4   5

45. I am willing to implement solutions
offered by others.   1   2   3   4   5

46. When I have to solve a problem,
I ask questions.   1   2   3   4   5

47. By setting a good example, I move
people to do good things.   1   2   3   4   5

48. I seek out conventional solutions to
problems as a last resort.   1   2   3   4   5

Source: Adapted and revised by D. Sousa from Goertz (2000).

Interpreting Your Score. The 48 questions are designed to elicit responses related to the eight categories of creative traits suggested by Goertz. To get a profile of how you perceived yourself in each of the eight areas, you will need to enter your responses in the following chart.

Directions. On the line to the right of each question, enter the number you circled as your response. Then add the six numbers across the row and put the total on the line in the Total Across Row column. (Note: The total for each row cannot exceed 30.)

You can judge the weight of your score as follows:

6–9: You see yourself as exhibiting this trait almost never.

10–14: You see yourself as exhibiting this trait seldom.

15–20: You see yourself as exhibiting this trait regularly.

21–25: You see yourself as exhibiting this trait frequently.

26–30: You see yourself as exhibiting this trait almost always.

						Total Across Row	Trait
1.__	9.__	17.__	26.__	34.__	41.__	_____	Passion for Work
10.__	16.__	24.__	33.__	39.__	43.__	_____	Independence
2.__	6.__	18.__	25.__	35.__	42.__	_____	Goal Setting
7.__	12.__	22.__	27.__	37.__	44.__	_____	Originality
3.__	11.__	20.__	28.__	36.__	45.__	_____	Flexibility
4.__	15.__	21.__	30.__	40.__	48.__	_____	Wide Range of Interests
8.__	13.__	19.__	29.__	32.__	46.__	_____	Intelligence
5.__	14.__	23.__	31.__	38.__	47.__	_____	Motivation

Reflections

Review the results above and answer the following questions:

- Were you surprised by your results? Why or why not?
- Are there some traits that you want to enhance? How will you go about doing that?

Tip 1.5: Learn How to Improve Your Memory

As of this writing, at least six different pharmaceutical companies are developing or testing drugs designed to enhance cognitive performance and improve memory recall in patients suffering from Alzheimer's disease and other conditions that affect memory. However, no available drugs or herbal supplements now exist that have been shown in reliable scientific studies to enhance memory in otherwise normal brains. If you want to improve your memory, you will have to rely for now on other tested techniques that work for most people. Here are a few tips that will help you to remember important information.

Remembering Names

Difficulty in remembering people's names is one of those mental tasks that can be improved with practice. The first rule of remembering anything is to pay attention and to repeatedly process the new learning—in this case, a person's name. You can become adept at remembering and recalling people's names if you are willing to put in the time and get into the habit of trying the following techniques.

Prominent Feature Association. When introduced, look for some prominent feature on the person. Start by studying the person's face closely for unusual features. Examine the eyes, eyebrows, chin, nose, forehead, mouth, complexion, and hairline. The goal here is to create an association between the facial feature and the name. Talk to yourself about the association. For example, "Darrell has lots of freckles" (remember Freckled Darrell). Look for other features as well. "Melinda is very tall" (remember Tall Melinda). The more bizarre the association, the more likely you are to remember it.

Name Association. Sometimes the person has a name that is the same or close to that of a famous person (Monroe, Ford) or someone else that you know. Associating the two names will help you remember them. You might also be able to associate the name with an occupation (Gardner, Singer), or with an animal (Fox, Swan), or a thing (Rose, Woods).

Repetition. After being introduced, use the person's name at least three times in your conversation (without overdoing it). "Hi, Darrell, nice to meet you. Do you have any kids, Darrell?" If the name is unusual, ask the person to spell it. Be sure to exchange business cards and say the name again as you look at the card. End your conversation with the person's name: "A real pleasure meeting you, Darrell." After the person leaves, repeat the name several times. If possible, find a spot where you can say it aloud, because auditory input improves remembering.

In all cases, quickly write down the person's name on your calendar, address book, program, agenda, or note pad and repeat it over the next few days. With practice and patience you will be surprised how well you will remember people's names. Keep in mind that few things will undermine a professional relationship more than when a person you have met several times realizes that you have not bothered to remember his or her name.

Other Memory Tips

Here are a few more tips that can help you remember material you need for your daily work or for a specific presentation. Some of these tips fall into the category of mnemonic (from the Greek "to remember") devices. These devices try to take advantage of the brain's predisposition for seeking out and remembering patterns.

- Keep your brain well nourished (refer to the suggestions at the beginning of this chapter). Avoid too much sugar and saturated fat. Eat green leafy vegetables. A 2004 study at the Massachusetts Institute of Technology showed that the magnesium found in these vegetables appears to help maintain memory.
- Get enough sleep. Too little sleep impairs concentration and increases irritability. Adequate sleep (usually eight hours or more per night) boosts your memory.
- Pay attention. Most memory problems come from lack of attention. Before you can remember anything, you must focus on it with the intent of remembering it. You will remember those things you decide to remember, mainly because you have a specific reason or motivation. Ask yourself, why do you want to learn this?
- Eliminate distractions while studying what you want to remember. For most people, the brain can give its full attention to only one major item at a time.
- Focus on understanding the main idea rather than memorizing isolated facts. Write down and repeat new information to help the brain transfer items from working memory to long-term memory.
- Form vivid, colorful mental images of things you want to remember. Use pleasant images as the brain often blocks unpleasant ones. Exaggerate the size of important parts of the image. Bizarre and humorous images are easier to remember.
- Link items together in an unusual story. Create a connection between the first and the next item. Then move on through the list linking each item with the next. Now fit these associations into a story. Keep the image as vivid as possible.
- To remember a list of items, try to make an acronym from the first letter of each important item in the list. For example, HOMES helps you remember the great lakes: Huron, Ontario, Michigan, Erie, and Superior. One trial attorney uses the acronym PIES to remember the four questions he asks to impeach

a witness: Prior convictions, Inconsistent prior statements, Evidence inconsistent with statements, and Statements that support his side.

- Recite the material aloud as though you were explaining it to somebody else. This increases your level of attention and helps to establish the neural connections needed to form the memory. All educators know that one of the best ways to learn and remember something is to teach it.

- Study in small doses. You tend to remember things that you study in short, intense sessions of 20 to 30 minutes. Longer sessions lead to fatigue and loss of attention—major enemies of memory. Allow at least a 10-minute break between sessions. At the end of each session, review what you have just studied. This is the time when the brain is most receptive to attaching sense and meaning to what you have learned, and thus more likely to store it in long-term memory. (See more about sense and meaning in chapter 3).

- Watch less television. Growing evidence suggests that watching too much television diminishes the brain's ability to focus on new learning.

- Avoid sustained stress. Researchers found that sustained high levels of stress activate chemicals that inhibit working memory and can damage the hippocampus (see the appendix), the part of the brain essential to long-term memory.

- Keep your brain challenged. Games and puzzles develop memory (Scrabble, crossword puzzles, and card games), strategizing (checkers and chess), and spatial skills (pool and pinball games). Learning another language or how to play a musical instrument are excellent ways to enhance memory.

Now that you know something about how your brain is organized, let's look at how you can use this information to make you more successful in your workplace.

Chapter 1— Understanding Your Brain

Key Points to Ponder

Use this page to jot down key points, ideas, strategies, and resources you want to consider later. This sheet is your personal journal summary and will help to jog your memory.

_____

_____

_____

_____

_____

_____

_____

CHAPTER 2

Using Your Brain in the Workplace

The brain is a wonderful organ: It starts working the moment you get up in the morning and does not stop until you get into the office.

—Robert Frost

Many books have been written about how to practice law, how to set up your office, and how to determine billable hours. But this book has a totally different perspective on where you work. In this chapter, we look at how to use some of the findings from brain research to improve the efficiency and effectiveness of your workplace. First, let's define the workplace as used here.

- If you are a **corporate law professional**, the workplace is your law firm's offices. Whether you are the sole boss, a partner, an associate, or paralegal, you need to understand the dynamics of the workplace and the influence that different thinking patterns have on your success and that of your firm. Even if you are the only lawyer in a one-person firm, members of your staff are also part of the workplace. What you do and how you do it affects their performance, motivation, and loyalty.
- If you are a **judge**, the workplace includes your chambers and courtroom. Although the courtroom is your realm, everything you do is watched by other courtroom personnel (e.g., bailiffs,

stenographers, defense lawyers, prosecutors, etc.), the media, spectators, jurors, your fellow judges, and appellate judges. Others will make judgments about your competence based partly on how you manage your courtroom and offices.

- For **law professors**, your work environment includes your office and the classroom. You are well aware that your reputation as a teacher is largely dependent on your students' perceptions of how you teach, what you teach, fairness, and your organizational skills. Additionally, your interactions with faculty colleagues, your habits of mind, and your publications all contribute to your persona and your success in the workplace.

TIP 2.1: Understand How Hemispheric Preferences Can Affect Your Workplace

Hemispheric preference affects your personality, your view of the world, how you interact with others, and your presentation style. In chapter 1, I explained the research on hemispheric specialization, and you had an opportunity to assess your own hemispheric preference. Other people whose degree of hemispheric preference is similar to yours are more likely to find you easy to understand and to work with. Conversely, those whose hemispheric preference is considerably different from yours will have difficulty understanding your views or approach to situations.

Implications of Hemispheric Preference

Let's examine two of the implications: How hemispheric preference can affect your workplace, and how it can influence your presentation style.

Managers and Leaders. Some researchers suggest that strongly left-hemisphere-preferred people make excellent managers because of their strengths in logic and analysis. They are strong on organization and procedures, produce highly detailed job descriptions, and generally run a tight ship. But this formal organization may be devoid of empathy and be overly protective. People who work in this office may not be motivated because there is no esprit de corps in the organization, and they feel underappreciated and are just putting in the hours in an impersonal establishment.

On the other hand, right-hemisphere-preferred individuals tend to make more effective leaders. They tend to run looser organizations where people work toward a common vision and feel valued for what they do. Effective leaders often have to think outside the box, persuade reluctant people, and find creative solutions to old problems. Strongly right-hemisphere-preferred individuals usually possess the charisma, empathy, and imagination to be successful in this role, even though they often feel overwhelmed by bureaucracy and details.

Many people possess the qualities of both left- and right-hemisphere preferences to some degree, but few excel in both.

Some researchers suggest that left-hemisphere-preferred people make better managers and right-hemisphere-preferred people make better leaders.

Bringing about Change. Managing a law firm or a courtroom today is a tough job; leading one is even tougher. Leaders need to be creative, ethical, inspiring, and respectful as well as knowledgeable about the law, methods of informing others, and social and cultural institutions. They have to articulate a clear vision to their colleagues. They should know how to identify and support areas that enhance the mission of the organization and modify those areas that impede it. If leaders are made and not born, how can you acquire the skills needed to be a leader and not just a manager? How will you use these skills to implement change?

It might seem strange to be discussing here how one can bring about change in the practice of law. But interpretation of the law is constantly affecting, and being affected by, societal changes. For example, different interpretations by the courts of the equal protection clause in the U.S. Constitution's Fourteenth Amendment have changed society dramatically in the nearly 140 years since the amendment was ratified.

Many people possess the qualities of both left- and right-hemisphere preferences, but few excel in both.

TIP 2.2: Use a Whole-Brain Leadership Approach to Bring About Change

The Cerebral Forces at Work. Cognitive processes, emotional relationships, and learning preferences will all influence an individual's thoughts and actions. Identifying specific components and how they interact can

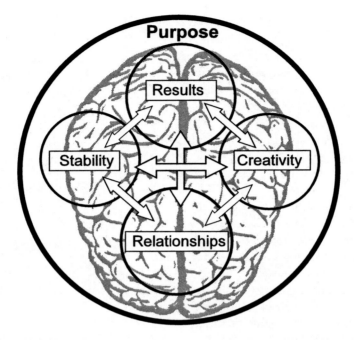

Figure 2.1 The four cerebral forces of creativity (right hemisphere), results (frontal lobe), relationships (emotional area), and stability (left hemisphere) interact in varying degrees, depending on the situation. Purpose (whole brain) integrates their influences to help the individual arrive at a final decision.

be helpful in examining and explaining leadership style in the workplace. There are many ways to categorize the cognitive and emotional functions of the brain. Researchers generally choose the model that will best fit their purposes. Based on what neuroscience knows so far, I suggest that people in positions of true leadership—those who see themselves primarily as change agents—are subject to the following five major cerebral forces influencing their thinking and behavior (see figure 2.1):

- **Creativity (more right-hemisphere situated).** Creativity describes the tendency to seek out alternatives for solving problems and taking action that contribute to survival, quality of life, and excellent performance. This force helps one explore options, think outside the box, support change, and clarify the vision of where to go next and in the future. It also embraces the notion of putting together ideas in law that everyone knows in new and different ways that are persuasive to others. Lawyers (and paralegals) may wonder, "What's a novel way to introduce this concept to the other members of this organization so that they will buy into it?" Judges (and their law clerks) may ask, "Is there a valid interpretation of this law that is more consistent with today's society?" Law professors may enquire, "Is there a better way to teach this critical concept that no one has thought of before?"

- **Stability (more left-hemisphere situated).** Stability refers to the tendency to retain and protect activities that bring stability, certainty, order, and logic to daily situations. This force helps one keep control over those resources that maintain balance and allow for a calm existence. The reality that most humans do not take well to change may attest to the power of this force. Leaders may wonder, "Will what I am contemplating bring about too much change at one time?" Judges may debate, "Is this decision really interpreting the law, or am I rewriting it?" Law professors might consider, "Will my suggestion for revamping this course upset the scope of the law school's curriculum?"

- **Relationships (likely centered in the emotional area).** Relationships explain why we seek out linkages and connections to others and avoid taking actions that undermine those relationships. This force influences one to rely on the loyalty and commitment of others to support initiatives. For a leader in a law firm, this becomes, "Am I alienating too many close colleagues with this decision?" For a judge, this may translate into, "How will my judicial colleagues react to this decision and could it affect their degree of support for future decisions?" For a law professor, this becomes, "Is my new approach to teaching this concept so radical that my colleagues could be irritated?"

- **Results (frontal lobe and emotional area).** Results refer to the tendency to get things done and to feel the satisfaction of accomplishment. This force enhances the positive feelings that come with closure. The leader in a law firm thinks, "We have been talking about this for years. Now we can make it happen." The judge supposes, "This has been a sticking point in law for a long time. Today I am going to settle it." For the law professor, it could be, "I have been working on this course revision for over a year. Today, it becomes reality."

- **Purpose (whole brain).** Purpose describes the tendency to justify any and all actions as being consistent with a life purpose, vision, and mission. This force tends to integrate all the other forces to

31

help one arrive at a final decision. To the leader, this notion says, "With this decision, we come closer to fulfilling our firm's mission." To the judge, it is, "I have always thought this was right. Today I get to explain why." For the law professor, "There is no doubt that this new course advances the study of the law into the twenty-first century."

These forces are independent but complementary parts of a whole-brain processing system, and they vary in intensity. They can act together in various combinations depending on the specific situation. How each force influences a given situation will often determine what skills and information a leader will use to solve a problem or handle conflict.

Let me give an example of how these forces interact. Faced with the deteriorating effectiveness of a colleague who is also a personal friend, a leader might avoid discussing poor job performance for fear of damaging a long-standing friendship. In this case, the relationship force, based primarily in the emotional area of the brain, wields greater influence than the results and stability forces that seek to maintain good lawyering. (As we will learn later in the book, emotional responses often override rational ones.) If the colleague's performance worsens, the leader could use creativity to design strategies that support the colleague in positive ways, thus lessening the chance that such action would adversely affect their personal relationship.

Personal Habits of Our Mind. The brain directs and controls the many different functions that affect how we think, decide, and act. Thus, our thinking style, learning preferences, creativity, intelligence, and personality traits enhance or hinder the influence of the cerebral forces. People who are gregarious and strong in interpersonal intelligence, for instance, are likely to be more influenced by the relationship force. Those who are stronger in logic may be influenced more by stability. Table 2.1 lists some of the personal habits of our mind that guide us through these cognitive and emotional processes, and the range of variations that exists in individuals.

As an example, take the concept of hemispheric preference. By using the instrument in chapter 1, individuals can assess their hemispheric preference as being more left brain, right brain, or balanced. Remember that these distinctions are more behavioral than physiological because not all functions associated with the left hemisphere are located on the left side and not all functions associated with the right hemisphere are located on the right side. Nonetheless, the descriptions of hemispheric preferences are useful in that they describe radically different ways of thinking. You will recall that a left-hemisphere-preferred person tends

TABLE 2.1 HABITS OF MIND THAT AFFECT DECISION MAKING		
Characteristic	**Varies From. . .**	**To**
Hemispheric Preference	(Left Preferred) Analytical, logical, linear	(Right Preferred) Holistic, intuitive, values-based
Working in a Group	Collaborative (high interpersonal intelligence)	Independent (high intrapersonal intelligence)
Evaluating Evidence	Analysis and logic	Emotions and values
Experiences	Abstract information as books, videos, and conversations	Interacting directly with people and things
Speed of Decision Making	Speedy, no matter the issue	Deliberate, well-thought-out process, no matter how urgent
Perspective	Focus on detail and data (high logical mathematical intelligence)	Looks at relationships that form the big picture (high visual-spatial intelligence)

to have a logical, sequential, and analytical approach to thinking that is substantially different from the right-hemisphere-preferred person, who has a holistic, intuitive, values-based approach.

Other important thinking style differences also exist. When gathering information or solving problems, some people prefer to collaborate, whereas others prefer to gather information and process it alone. Some people evaluate evidence based on logic and analysis, whereas others rely more on emotions and values to guide their decisions. How we experience the world also differs among us. Some people prefer an abstract approach, collecting experiences through books, videos, and discussions. Others want to interact directly with their environment and get firsthand experiences. In other words, the former prefers to watch the vacation videos produced by the latter. Furthermore, how quickly people make decisions and their perspectives on data are also variables that influence cognitive processes.

Whenever leaders (or anyone else for that matter) make decisions, all these cerebral forces are at hand, subconsciously directing which skills are brought into play and influencing what information is used or ignored in the decision-making process. By being aware of these forces and the role each one plays as well as their own thinking preferences, leaders are more apt to make decisions that are ethical and supportive of their organization's mission.

Leaders should assess the thinking styles of the people they are responsible for by using a validated diagnostic instrument. Such an instrument is far more reliable and thorough than the subjective impressions of even the most observant of leaders. Many of these tools are commercially available and can be found online. They offer the leadership team a valuable opportunity to discuss their thinking preferences. It is important, however, to remember the following:

- Preferences are neither good nor bad, but are assets or liabilities, depending on the situation.
- Distinctive preferences emerge early in life and tend to remain stable through the years.
- We can expand our repertoire of preferences so that we can act outside our preferred style, but it is difficult.
- Understanding the mind preferences of others makes communication and collaboration easier.
- Most of us tend to seek out jobs whose work requirements are most compatible with our mind style.
- People can function and survive in jobs whose work requirements are vastly different from their mind style, but they are usually under considerable stress.

TIP 2.3: Hire People Whose Thinking Patterns Are Different from Your Own

From Thought to Action

When individuals identify their thinking styles, they gain insight into how their preferences unconsciously guide the way they behave, lead, and communicate with others. Their actions may encourage or stifle desirable behaviors in others. When working in a group, for instance, a left-brain-thinking leader who reveals a step-by-step suggestion for solving a problem will probably suppress the flow of creative ideas from right-brain thinkers. On the other hand, a right-brain leader whose meetings lack structure to encourage openness and creative thought may unsettle those left-brain thinkers who need time to process ideas and search for logical solutions. In both cases, the leaders are inadvertently stifling the very creativity they seek in others. It is equally important for the right-brain creative leader to recognize the contributions of the logical thinkers as it is for the left-brain leader to acknowledge the ideas of the visionaries.

Embracing Different Thinkers. Once leaders have gained an understanding into their personal thinking and leadership styles, they need to hire and interact regularly with people whose thinking styles are quite different from their own. This is no easy task, because we generally prefer to be around those who think and act as we do, thereby raising our comfort level. When we discuss a problem with people who think like us, they are apt to agree with our position and not offer any out-of-the-box idea that radically differs from that view. Although our ego is stroked by this validation, no new ideas come into the mix for consideration.

Suppose, on the other hand, we discuss the problem with someone whose thought patterns are different from our own. It may be difficult at first to get past the widely varying perspectives. But the feedback is likely to reveal new options that will improve the quality of our decision making. These individuals often offer ideas that complement our weaknesses and exploit our strengths. Leaders make better decisions when they are forced to look at all sides of an issue and entertain potential solutions that their thinking style might have rejected.

We discussed earlier that when trying to talk others into action, we should tailor our mode of delivery to that of the listener. Some people respond better to graphic presentations, while others prefer stories and anecdotes. Still others get their information by digesting statistics and facts. The point is to use the preferred learning modality of the recipient—rather than your own—to ensure meaningful and accurate communication.

> *Leaders make better decisions when forced to entertain potential solutions their own thinking style might have rejected.*

TIP 2.4: Create Whole-Brained Teams

Teams in the Workplace

Although professional firms of doctors and lawyers often start out in a collegial atmosphere, if each member's productivity and compensation are measured primarily in billable hours and other fees, they eventually can turn into negative environments. Competition, conflict, and insecurity emerge, producing a stressful workplace that undermines the organization's mission and effectiveness. One way to avoid this negative result is to form teams that work together on a particular case or project. In a workplace with few members, the whole office can be the team.

Teams can make important contributions in transforming an organization's culture, implementing change, or generating a fresh approach to an age-old legal interpretation. Take, for example, the challenges faced in adapting older legal doctrines developed for one technology, such as radio and television, to the modern Internet.

> *Team members should represent a broad range of thinking styles, thereby encouraging a whole-brained approach to the problem.*

When creating teams, take care to avoid homogeneity of thought. Although homogeneous teams will function efficiently, the number of proposed solutions or creative opportunities will be limited. Most problem solving requires looking at the situation both analytically and holistically, not just one way or the other.

Leaders should strive to include on a team individuals representing a broad range of thinking styles, thereby encouraging a whole-brained approach to the problem. In this environment, people cross-fertilize the ideas of others, thereby providing a range of potential and innovative solutions. This will not come easily to the team because members do not naturally understand one another. Thus, when the team is deliberating, the leader has to manage the creative process by getting members to acknowledge their differences and, if needed, devise guidelines for working together before they tackle the problem at hand.

Establishing rules about how to work together can seem silly to an adult group of law professionals whose members have had years of experience in dealing with people. But work teams often stagnate because most people tend to value politeness over truth, avoid emotional topics, and opt out of discussions if their proposals are not appreciated.

Conflict may arise because people who do not understand the cognitive perspectives of others can get irritated. Disagreements may become personal. In this situation, the leader should depersonalize the conflict and defuse the anger by noting that differences of opinion do not indicate stubbornness but merely represent another perspective. No one thinking style is inherently better than any other. Rather, each style brings a uniquely valuable perspective to the discussion, allowing all team members to assess a variety of options and solutions.

Forming Effective Teams

Highly trained professionals, such as lawyers, judges, and law professors, recognize that they possess specialized knowledge and skills. This mind-set prompts them to closely protect their autonomy of practice. Although they may recognize the value of team input, they seldom are willing to make the individual concessions that are sometimes necessary for the good of the whole organization. To ensure that your teams function effectively, consider the following checklist of strategies when forming teams in the workplace:

- Include members who have the expertise to contribute positively to the team's mission. Because cohesiveness is so crucial to success, including a member who refuses to reach consensus, or who attacks others personally, can undermine or hamper the team's work.
- The mission should be clear. Every member should be able to answer the question, "Why am I here?"
- Team members should understand their roles and responsibilities. It is wise to have a facilitator (or team leader), a recorder, and one who observes and gives feedback on group processing.
- The team should establish ground rules for its operation, such as a specific agenda, starting and ending times, and serious efforts to eliminate interruptions while meeting.
- The team should adopt a mechanism for resolving differences of opinion, such as finding a compromise, imposing majority rule, or tabling the issue for later discussion.
- The team should formulate a strategy for dealing with personal conflicts that arise during the team's meeting, such as one person dominating the discussion or blocking decision making.
- The team should adopt measures that periodically monitor the progress of the team toward reaching its goals.
- The team should ensure that outcomes and deadlines are clearly explained.
- Consider hiring a professional consultant to train members in how teams should work. Part of the culture of a team includes discussing the structure of their process and work. This training can enhance communication skills as well as show the team how to reach consensus, respect the opinions of others, and advocate their decisions to other constituencies.

37

How Teams Fail. Teams are likely to fail when the members do not clearly understand the team's mission, fail to buy into the team's purpose or goals, and do not understand or carry out their roles and responsibilities. Sometimes, team members do not realize the processes needed to work as a team, such as building consensus, listening, and accepting the opinions of those they disagree with.

Teams in the Courtroom

Lawyer teams can be incredibly effective in the courtroom for several reasons. If you are the lead trial lawyer, you can get so wrapped up in the content and delivery of your presentation that you may miss important clues or nuances during testimony. These clues may come from a witness, the defendant, or the jurors. Team members can be assigned to watch specific people. Their feedback provides new information and a fresh perspective that you otherwise might not have considered.

Team members can use Internet access to get important documents or other resources from the home office while you continue your presentation. For reasons mentioned earlier, include colleagues who represent a variety of thinking styles. Of course, the teams should not be so large as to overwhelm the court.

TIP 2.5: Control the Amount of Stress in the Workplace

Everyone is under some degree of pressure in the workplace. Sometimes, external pressures are a positive factor, helping people to be more productive. Some people actually thrive under short-term added pressure, and they often say that stress is a good thing because it brings excitement to their work. The human body is designed to meet these temporary demands. Granted, many people who get excited by working hard in a manageable way toward an achievable goal are happy, but they also are not under continuous stress as defined here.

> *Stress is a health risk. Be prepared to deal with your own stress and the stress in your colleagues if you want an effective workplace.*

Stress is a health risk, and excessive and prolonged stress can take its toll. When under stress, the body releases a substance called cortisol, a steroid that affects the brain's performance, including motor coordination, concentration, learning, and memory. Ironically, stress at work can lead to a serious risk of litigation, carrying significant liabilities for damages, unwanted publicity, and loss of reputation.

Stress is caused by a variety of factors, not all of which are work related. Some stress is caused by conditions at home or by personal health problems that are independent of the workplace. Among the most common causes of work-related stress are the following:

- Working long or inflexible hours
- Excessive time away from home and family
- Confusion about duties and responsibilities
- Lack of job security
- Conflict among colleagues
- Harassment of all types
- Lack of control over work, sense of powerlessness
- Excessive time pressures
- Continual unreasonable demands in performance
- Poor attempts at communication and conflict resolution

Stress in the workplace is a reality. Your goal should be to manage stress by becoming aware of how you respond to it—in your colleagues and in yourself.

Dealing with Stress in Others

If you recognize stress in a colleague, do something about it, especially if you are that person's supervisor. If you cannot handle the situation, identify someone who can. Later, discuss with the colleague the work-related factors that caused the stress. Then determine what you can do to moderate those factors. Do not assume that the situation will automatically improve or hope that the colleague will become more resilient. Because the continuing presence of cortisol in the bloodstream will undermine emotional stability, it is more likely that things will get worse. If you cannot eliminate the cause of the colleague's stress, consider removing the person from the situation causing the stress. Share with this person the techniques you use to deal with your own stress and, if needed, suggest appropriate counseling.

Dealing with Your Own Stress

Your daily life is likely filled with hectic, disjointed, and tense situations that often require immediate decisions and conflict resolution. Maintaining this frenzied pace takes a toll on your mental equilibrium, upsetting the delicate balance of compassion and justice that you need to make sound decisions. Here are a few suggestions for dealing with constant stress to restore your focus and sense of inner peace.

- **Start your day off peacefully.** Use silence, soothing music, reflection, or meditation to start your day.
- **Learn to be mindful.** Mindfulness means avoiding an instant response to a situation and giving yourself time to determine all the options you have available before acting.
- **Slow things down.** If a group or meeting is moving too fast, slow yourself down by sitting back, reflecting, and taking a deep breath.
- **Create your own measures.** Create personal measures you can use to determine whether you are becoming a better person and colleague. These measures help you evaluate positive changes in your behavior, such as getting angry less, or becoming more patient.
- **Expect surprise.** Accept surprise as a fact of life and do not get thrown by it.
- **Practice gratefulness.** Find the time to count your blessings and be grateful for what you have. Expressing your gratefulness to colleagues can improve professional relationships dramatically.
- **Take time to exercise.** When under stress, find time to stretch and go for a walk. Physical exercise brings more oxygenated blood to the brain, stoking your decision-making processes. Vigorous exercise burns up adrenaline and releases pleasure-producing chemicals called endorphins, thereby lowering your stress level.
- **Watch your diet.** People under stress often avoid eating, making them even more susceptible to stress factors. Eat and drink healthfully. As mentioned in chapter 1, be sure to take your vitamins, especially the B group, which protect against stress susceptibility and depression. Vitamin C is also important because it helps maintain the immune system, which is often compromised during periods of high stress. At the same time, avoid excessive alcohol, tobacco, and caffeine, all of which increase stress levels.
- **Maintain a life outside work.** Be sure you get involved in activities outside work that will help you to meet new people. Find ways to have fun by starting a creative hobby that will take your mind away from work worries and remind you that there is more to life than the office.
- **Talk to others.** Confiding in trusted friends or relatives is a useful way to articulate worries and negative feelings. It can give a fresh perspective and help to make stressful situations more manageable.

In most organizations, stress is an inevitable companion. To some degree, that is desirable. Without challenges and pressures, work lacks excitement and meaning. But we all have the capacity to be overwhelmed by work-related stress and to experience its exhausting and unhealthy effects. Don't let that happen to you.

TIP 2.6: Remember That Laughter Is Powerful Medicine

The Benefits of Humor

Humor has many benefits when used frequently and appropriately in the workplace and in other settings. For the skeptics, here are some of the physiological and psychological benefits of using humor.

> *Humor has many benefits when used frequently and appropriately in the workplace.*

Physiological Benefits. The following are the physiological benefits of humor:

- **More oxygen.** You know that the brain needs oxygen for fuel. When we laugh, we get more oxygen in the bloodstream, so the brain is better fueled. That means we are likely to use our thought processes more effectively.
- **Endorphin surge.** Laughter causes the release of endorphins into the bloodstream. Endorphins are the body's natural pain-killers, and they also give you a feeling of euphoria. In other words, you enjoy the moment in body as well as in mind. Endorphins counteract the negative effects of cortisol that may be present because of stress. Furthermore, endorphins also stimulate the brain's memory systems, so you are more likely to remember what you are mentally processing (and learning) while laughing.
- **Other benefits.** Laughter reduces your blood pressure, stimulates the immune system, and relaxes tense muscles.

Psychological and Sociological Benefits. The following are the psychological and sociological benefits of humor:

- **Gets attention.** The first thing you have to do when starting a presentation is to get the listener to focus. Because the normal human brain loves to laugh, starting with a humorous tale (such as a joke, pun, or story) gets attention. Humor should not be limited to an opening joke or story. Because of its value as an attention-getter and retention strategy, look for ways to use humor periodically within the context of your presentation.

41

- **Creates a positive climate.** When people laugh together, they bond, and a community spirit emerges—all positive forces for a climate conducive to working together and learning.
- **Increases retention.** We know that emotions enhance retention, so the positive feelings that result from laughter increase the probability that the listeners will remember what they learned.
- **Improves everyone's mental health.** Law offices and courthouses and all their occupants are under more stress than ever. Taking time to laugh can relieve that stress and give the staff a better mental attitude with which to accomplish their tasks. We can take our work seriously, but ourselves lightly.
- **Is an effective management tool.** Good-natured humor (not teasing or sarcasm) can be an effective way of reminding employees and colleagues of their responsibilities without raising tension in the workplace. Leaders who use appropriate humor are more likeable, and fellow workers have a more positive feeling toward them. Furthermore, they set an example by showing that appropriate humor and laughter are acceptable. Laughter adds life to your years and years to your life.

> *Laughter adds life to your years and years to your life.*

Avoid Personal Sarcasm

All of the wonderful benefits mentioned above are the result of using wholesome humor that everyone can enjoy, rather than sarcasm aimed at a colleague, which is inevitably destructive to someone. Sarcasm reveals contempt and insensitivity and can reinforce stereotypes by singling out a particular person or group. Even some well-intentioned leaders say, "Oh, I know my colleagues very well, so they can take sarcasm. They know I'm only kidding." That line of reasoning led Thomas Carlyle to view sarcasm as "the language of the devil; for which reason, I have long since as good as renounced it." More than ever, today's workplaces are under stress and people come to their job looking for moral and emotional support. Sarcasm is one of the factors that undermines that support and turns workers against their peers and the organization. Besides, there are plenty of sources of good humor without personal sarcasm.

TIP 2.7: Walk around the Room to Make Better Decisions

Sitting slows your thinking. When you sit for more than 30 minutes, the blood in your body begins to pool in two places: your feet and your seat.

Blood that is pooled is not doing your brain any good. Once you get up and start walking, your calf muscles alternately contract and relax, breaking up these pools. In less than a minute of walking, you will have about 15 percent more blood in the brain. That means 15 percent more oxygen and glucose, thereby increasing the brain's fuel supply and efficiency.

Walking around pumps about 15 percent more blood to the brain than sitting at your desk.

If you have to ask important questions or make decisions, do not remain seated. Above all, do not sit with your feet on the desk because now the blood is going to the part of your body that ought not be making the decision. Instead, get up and move around while thinking through your decision.

As for the telephone, get yourself a cordless model or a 25-foot-long phone cord so that you can pace while talking. Once again, moving around increases blood flow to the brain and increases the likelihood that you will make a better decision. We do think better on our feet than on our seat!

Chapter 2— Using Your Brain in the Workplace

Key Points to Ponder

Use this page to jot down key points, ideas, strategies, and resources you want to consider later. This sheet is your personal journal summary and will help to jog your memory.

_____

_____

_____

_____

_____

_____

_____

CHAPTER 3

Applying Brain Research to Your Practice

The law must be stable, but it must not stand still.

—Roscoe Pound

Now that we have discussed ways of making use of brain research in your workplace, let's look at how that research can affect your practice of law. This chapter discusses some of the most important findings about how people learn, including the power of graphics, the time of day when people are most alert to learning, the amount of information they can process at one time, and the impact of emotions on learning. I offer suggestions as to how the research can guide the design, delivery, and length of your presentations.

Not all suggestions are appropriate for all venues. If you are a lawyer working with clients in your office, you can present information in just about any way you want—with only your imagination as the limit. In the courtroom, however, you obviously encounter certain restraints. Nonetheless, few lawyers really take advantage of all they can do, even within the limits of those restraints, to lay out a powerful, novel, and memorable presentation to judges and jurors.

If you are a judge, you probably have considerable leeway in deciding how you want to present your instructions to the jury, although what you say has likely been put into a standardized format and may be subject to scrutiny by the trial attorneys. Some of the suggestions in this chapter are appropriate for you, because you still have to be concerned with how much you can tell jurors at one time. You also will want to consider which methods of presentation are likely to make your instructions to jurors worth remembering.

As a law professor, the suggestions in this chapter offer plenty of applications to your teaching. You may already be incorporating these techniques in your classes. If so, I suspect students find your classes among the more stimulating ones they attend. Lawyers I have interviewed have often remarked about the tedium in lecture classes compared with the pleasure of those classes that were interactive, multisensory, and full of sense and meaning, and occasionally, humor.

TIP 3.1: Keep Sensory Preferences in Mind When Planning Your Presentations

Implications of Sensory Preferences to Presentation Style

In chapter 1, we discussed the importance of knowing your sensory preferences because they are part of your learning style, and your learning style greatly influences how you present information to a client, a judge, or a jury. Obviously, other people's sensory preferences can be very different from yours, and some can be very similar. Here are a few essential things to remember:

- People with different sensory preferences will behave differently during learning. A 6- to 12-member jury is likely to have a broad mix of sensory preferences, so you have to be prepared to address them all.
- Recognize that you will innately present information to others in a way that favors your own sensory preferences. If you are a strong auditory learner, for example, you prefer to "stand and deliver" when presenting. Lecturing is your favorite instructional method. People in your audience who are also strong auditory learners will feel comfortable with this style and learn much from you. Visually preferred learners, however, can have difficulty in maintaining focus throughout all this talk. Their attention will drift, and they will doodle or look at other materials to satisfy their visual appetite.
- If you have a strong visual preference, then you will likely show lots of graphics during your presentations. Visual learners, of course, will be at ease with this approach. On the other hand,

46

individuals with auditory preferences want to talk about what they are learning, and they can become frustrated with presenters who use primarily visual strategies. (Ever notice jurors appearing like they desperately want to ask you a question? These are very likely auditorily preferred learners.) These auditory learners will also be sensitive to various elements of your voice, such as pitch, rhythm, tone, timbre, inflection, and loudness. Varying these elements during your presentation will keep these listeners' attention.

> *Your sensory preferences strongly influence your presentation style.*

- Learners with strong kinesthetic preferences require movement while learning or they become restless—tapping their pencils, squirming in their seats, or (if they can) walking around the room. Because judges and jurors are trapped in their chairs, their frustration of not being able to move will erode their attention span. You can relieve their frustrations somewhat by keeping yourself in motion within the presentation area and by using your arms to make broad gestures that emphasize your words. In effect, this allows them to channel their kinesthetic needs vicariously through you. Corny as it sounds, it works.

  Law professors should realize that more than one-third of today's students have kinesthetic preferences. To keep their attention, have the class get up and move at least 10 steps about every 20 to 30 minutes and have them share what they have just learned with a partner. Not only does this "think, pair, share" movement appease the kinesthetic learners, but it also gets everyone's blood moving, bringing more oxygen and glucose to brain cells. Furthermore, talking about what you have just learned increases the chances of remembering it.

- Because your own sensory preferences have such a strong influence on your presentation style, design your presentations to include activities to address all sensory preferences and learning styles. Do you have enough graphics, and are they clear and not argumentative? Are you using vocabulary that non-lawyers can understand? Can you emphasize your points with body language and movement that complement, but do not distract, from what you are saying?

47

Important Caution. You may be wondering whether you can determine a potential juror's learning style by asking certain questions during voir dire. The answer is no. Determining almost any aspect of a person's learning style with accuracy requires answering numerous research-validated questions on a written instrument, followed by an analysis and, if possible, a one-on-one interview. Don't try to accomplish this during voir dire, and don't worry about it either. Just be sure to include all the components that we mentioned here in your presentations, where appropriate.

TIP 3.2: Design Your Presentations to Address the Whole Brain

What Does Presenting to the Whole Brain Mean?

General Guidelines. Although the two hemispheres process information differently, we learn best when both are engaged during learning. Therefore, design your presentations to include activities directed at both hemispheres so that your listeners can integrate the new learning into a meaningful whole. Here are some ways to do that.

- Deal with Concepts Verbally and Visually. When presenting new concepts, alternate discussion with visual models. Use a board or an image projector to show illustrations, charts, time lines, and graphs that encourage your listeners to visually organize information and relationships. (An in-depth discussion of various graphic organizers appears later in this chapter.) Write on a poster board or computer screen the key words that represent the concept and then use a simple diagram to show relationships among the key ideas within and between concepts. This approach helps listeners attach both auditory and visual cues to the information, increasing the likelihood that sense and meaning will emerge. If you plan to include material from a videotape or digital video, show the smallest segment that has the maximum meaning and then stop the tape and discuss what was shown.

  Although you make these presentations in your opening and closing statements, your witnesses also may need to have graphics available to help listeners understand their testimony. For example, suppose a witness who is a government informant is testifying about conversations recorded on an audiotape with several defendants. A chart with the names and photographs (if appropriate) of the people whose voices are heard on the tape will help jurors and the judge know who is speaking at any given time. Use a chart also to explain slang expressions and terms on the audiotape that jurors are not likely to know.

- Position of Items on Visual Aids Can Suggest Relationships. Position information on a visual aid so that the brain's right hemisphere discerns the correct relationship between concepts and ideas. Use vertical positioning to imply a step or time sequence, or hierarchy. Thus, writing

> *Delaware*
> *Pennsylvania*
> *New Jersey*

is appropriate to indicate the order of these states' admission into the Union (chronology).

On the other hand, writing them horizontally implies a parallel relationship, such as

> *Delaware, Pennsylvania, New Jersey*

to identify any three eastern states with dense population. Avoid writing information in visual aids haphazardly whenever a parallel or hierarchical relationship among the elements is important for your listeners to remember.

For example, if you need to show the jury that a defendant could be convicted of any one of three crimes of different severity, list the crimes vertically, in the order of most to least severe. Including a number also helps the jurors remember the sequence of severity, such as

(1) Second-degree murder
(2) Voluntary manslaughter
(3) Involuntary manslaughter

- Discuss Concepts Logically and Intuitively. Present concepts from both logical and intuitive perspectives. That means you start with concrete information and then proceed to possible implications. For example, if you are presenting the circumstances surrounding a serious motor vehicle accident, talk about the factual (logical) events first, such as the individuals involved, injuries incurred, weather conditions, and so forth. When you believe the listeners understand these concepts, move on to more thought-provoking (intuitive) notions, such as asking the listeners to think about the financial and emotional impact that the severe injuries have had on the victims and their families.

49

- Avoid Conflicting Messages. Make sure that your words, tone, and pacing match your gestures, facial expressions, and body language. The brain's left hemisphere interprets words literally, but the right hemisphere evaluates body language, tone, and content. If the two hemispheric interpretations are inconsistent, the mind generates a conflict message. As a result, the listener withdraws internally to resolve the conflict and is no longer focused on your presentation.

  If, for example, you are making statements of fact but have a quizzical look on your face and an informal stance, listeners may become confused about what to believe.

- Clear Away Irrelevant Visuals. When visuals, such as poster boards, are no longer needed, clear them away. Doing so reduces the chance that previous and unrelated word cues will become associated with the new topic under discussion. This problem relates particularly to listeners with strong visual preferences. Also, make sure that any visuals presented by your opponents are cleared from sight before you begin your presentation.

In the courtroom, make sure any visuals presented by your opponent are cleared from sight before you begin your presentation.

Have a Backup Plan

Modern technology is great—when it works. Computers and overhead and digital image projectors are all subject to glitches that can ruin a presentation. What will you do if the technology fails? Getting flustered and agitated will hardly instill confidence in your clients or other listeners. Have a backup plan that can be put in place quickly. When preparing an important presentation, ask yourself: "How can I still get my information across effectively even if something goes wrong with the technology?"

Your options include having a second set of equipment on hand, that is, a backup laptop computer or image projector. Another possibility is to have the presentation duplicated on less sophisticated technology. For example, if your

Modern technology can break down. Always have a backup plan for your presentation.

computer setup fails, having your presentation also on acetate sheets means that you can continue with just an overhead projector. Still another alternative is to have the presentation copied onto poster boards that can be brought in quickly to replace the broken equipment. If all else fails, ask for a recess and get replacement equipment fast.

TIP 3.3: Use Graphic Organizers to Make Your Points

We have all heard the maxim that "a picture is worth a thousand words." Patent lawyers recognize the importance of detailed diagrams when submitting patent applications. Yet many legal documents often contain hundreds of pages of written text, but rarely a diagram. Even lawyers writing these documents can get lost in their own narration, not realizing that a simple diagram could easily reduce confusion.

This is where graphic organizers come in.

Graphic Organizers. Graphic organizers are diagrams that illustrate the relationships between and among facts, concepts, and events. Showing, as opposed to just telling, can be a powerful way to improve understanding and to help your listeners remember important information. Graphic organizers are effective for the following reasons.

> *Graphic organizers are powerful memory devices that prove a picture is worth a thousand words.*

- Spatial arrangements that show the information's structure reduce the language demands necessary to understand the information. Thus, graphic organizers are particularly effective with people (like clients and jurors) who do not have strong linguistic abilities and who rely more on visual (i.e., nonlinguistic) representations for their comprehension.
- Graphic organizers also help the observers separate what is essential to know from what might be interesting, but unimportant, information. This is particularly important in law school classes where students often have difficulty deciding how much of the enormous amount of material is worth remembering.
- Because the language demands on the observers are reduced, you can often use diagrams to address the concepts at a more sophisticated level of thought.

There are many different kinds of graphic organizers. Computer programs, such as Inspiration Software, can help you construct graphic organizers in just a few minutes. The secret is to pick the organizer that most accurately represents the relationships you want your listeners and observers to remember as a result of your presentation. The following are some common types of organizers:

- Spider maps
- Venn diagrams
- Pie charts
- Bar graphs
- Time lines
- Process and cause-effect diagrams
- Episode patterns

General Guidelines. Regardless of which graphic organizer you choose, consider these general guidelines when constructing them:

- Use the fewest words and symbols to carry the message. People with low visual preference can become confused by complicated graphics and will spend too much time trying to decode them.
- Keep the vocabulary as simple as possible. Otherwise, those with low auditory preference will ponder the meaning of unknown words thereby losing the rest of what you are saying.
- Link related branches with arrows. If observers do not see the relationships clearly, they are likely to make up their own.
- Use the same color for related branches and different colors for different branches. This technique helps observers to separate the various components visually without becoming confused.
- Make central lines thicker than subtopic lines. This helps your observers recognize the levels of a hierarchy.
- Emphasize key words and symbols. Use highlighting and bold and larger fonts to emphasize key points.
- Always write text upright or, if necessary, at a slight angle. People with low visual preference or poor eyesight will often ignore printed text that is turned sideways.
- Use images instead of words, where appropriate.
- Present facts and avoid argumentative interpretations. Many of these guidelines hold true for diagrams that you or a witness may generate in the courtroom. Practicing these guidelines will help ensure that they are followed. Of course, be sure to comply with the rules of discovery and remember to mark each diagram for identification. Examples of some of the most common types of graphic organizers are shown on the following pages.

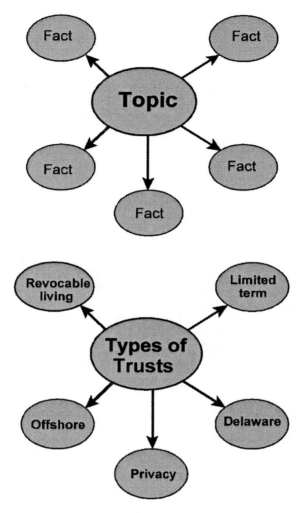

Figure 3.1 This is an example of a spider map. It is best used to show examples of a central theme—in this case, examples of different types of trusts.

Spider Maps. Spider maps show examples of a main idea (see figure 3.1). The main theme is written in the center and the examples are written in the outlying ovals.

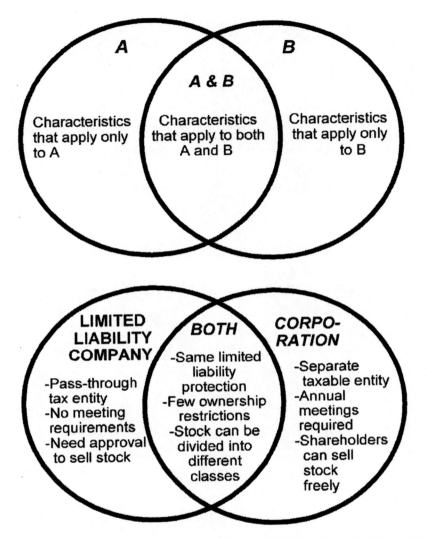

Figure 3.2 This Venn diagram compares the similarities and differences between a limited liability company and a corporation.

Venn Diagrams. Venn diagrams are useful for showing the similarities and differences between two (or three) items (see figure 3.2). The common characteristics are written in the area where the two circles overlap. Characteristics outside the overlapped area are called the critical attributes of that concept. Critical attributes are discussed later.

Money Acquired from Victims

During 2002-2004

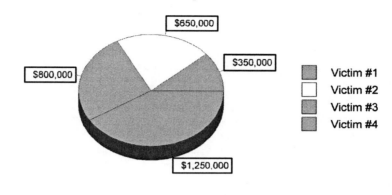

Money Spent by Defendant

During 2003-2004

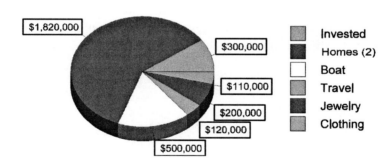

Figure 3.3 Pie charts show the relative proportion of variables to a whole. In this example, the charts show clearly the amount of money the defendant took from each victim and how that money was spent.

Pie Charts. Pie charts are among the easiest graphics to understand because the slices of the pie are drawn to represent the relative value of a category to the whole (see figure 3.3).

	2002	2003	2004
Victim #1	150,000	100,000	100,000
Victim #2	300,000	200,000	150,000
Victim #3	400,000	300,000	100,000
Victim #4	500,000	400,000	350,000

Figure 3.4 Bar graphs are useful for representing information that is discontinuous over time. In this example, the bar chart shows the amount acquired by the defendant from each victim over a three-year period.

Bar Graphs. These graphs are best for showing one-time items that are not continuous and that occur over a period of time (see figure 3.4). Bars demonstrate the relative size of different items at certain intervals. Each bar represents a specific quantity, and multiple bars may be grouped and displayed vertically or horizontally.

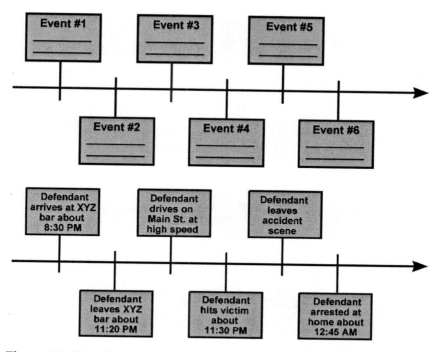

Figure 3.5 Time lines help your observers recognize the chronology of events. This example uses the time-line form to explain the sequence of events in a hit-and-run case.

Time Lines. In complicated cases, it is often difficult for your listeners to keep track of the time sequence of events. Time-line organizers help to illustrate the chronology of an incident (see figure 3.5).

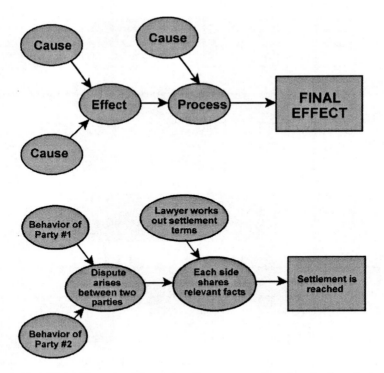

Figure 3.6 This diagram illustrates the process involved when two parties have a dispute requiring a settlement. Each party's behavior (cause) results in a dispute (effect). A third party (usually a lawyer) proposes the terms of a settlement that each party reviews and may amend until a settlement is reached (final effect).

Process and Cause-Effect Diagrams (Simple). Process and cause-effect diagrams are useful to illustrate both simple and complex cause-effect relationships and the processes associated with them that will achieve a specific outcome (see figure 3.6).

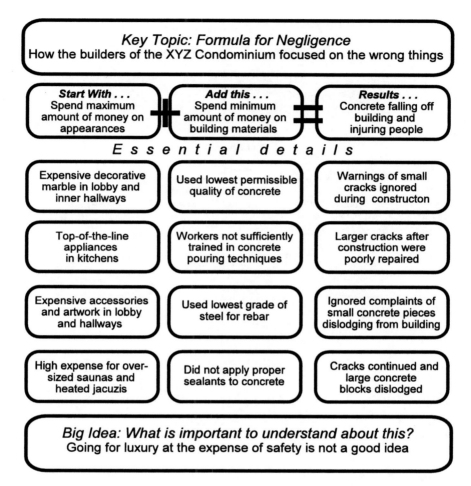

Figure 3.7 It is sometimes necessary to use a chart to show a complex series of cause-and-effect relationships. In this example, all the elements and details of a complex liability case are brought together in this one visual representation.

Process and Cause-Effect Diagrams (Complex). These more complex diagrams should be used with caution. Process and cause-effect diagrams for complex situations are also possible, but carefully limit their use to avoid overwhelming the observers (see figure 3.7).

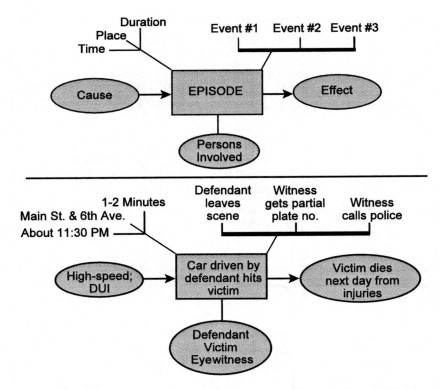

Figure 3.8 This episode pattern illustrates the significant events surrounding the hit-and-run case that is also the subject of the time line in Figure 3.5.

Episode Patterns. Episode patterns organize information about specific events by plotting place, time, and duration as well as the people involved, significant events, and a particular cause and effect (see figure 3.8).

How Memory Works

In your practice, you often expect people to remember important information that you tell them. You will be surprised how much people will remember what you say, if you know and apply some basic facts about how the human memory system works. Figure 3.9 shows the major components of our memory systems.

Immediate Memory. Our senses are constantly picking up the sights, smells, sounds, and other data from our environment. All of this information has to be screened by the brain to determine its importance.

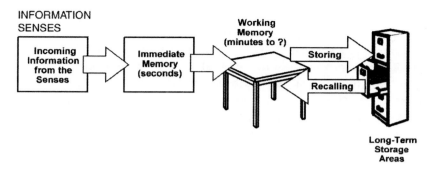

Figure 3.9 A simplified diagram of how memory works. Information from the senses passes through immediate memory to working memory for processing. With sufficient review, it may move into long-term storage.

Incoming sensory data move to the first of two temporary memories, called immediate memory. The immediate memory area is a place where we put information briefly until we make a quick decision on how to dispose of it. Immediate memory can hold data for up to about 30 seconds, but it usually dispenses with most data in less than a second. The individual's experiences determine the data's importance. If the information is of little or no importance within this time frame, it drops out of the memory system. For example, when you look up the telephone number of the local pizza parlor for the first time, you usually can remember it just long enough to make the call. After that, the number is of no further importance to you and it fades out of immediate memory. The next time you call for pizza, you will have to look up that number again.

Working Memory. Working memory is the second temporary memory and the place where conscious processing occurs. In figure 3.9, working memory is represented as a work table, a place of limited capacity where we can build, take apart, or rework ideas for eventual storage somewhere else. When something is in working memory, it generally demands our attention.

Capacity of Working Memory. Working memory can handle only a few items at one time. This capacity limit changes with age. Preadolescents can handle three to seven items, with an average of five. Through adolescence the capacity increases to a range of five to nine, with

> *Most people can handle only about seven items in working memory at any one time. We cannot recall what we have not stored.*

61

an average of seven. For most people, that number remains constant throughout life. This may explain why many items in human history are grouped by sevens: the seven seas, the seven deadly sins, the seven virtues, the seven notes of the musical scale, the seven ages of man, the seven days of the week, and the seven wonders of the world.

Let's test this notion. Get a pencil and a piece of paper. A timer will also help. When ready, stare at the following number for seven seconds, then look away and write it down. Ready? Go.

9170532

Check the number you wrote down. Chances are you got it right. Let's try it again with the same rules. Stare at the new number below for seven seconds, then look away and write it down. Ready? Go.

4915082637

Again, check the number you wrote down. Did you get all 10 of the digits in the correct sequence? Probably not. Because the digits were random, you had to treat each digit as a single item, and your working memory just ran out of capacity. This limited capacity explains why we have to memorize a song or a poem in stages. We start with the first group of lines by repeating them frequently (a process called rehearsal). Then we memorize the next lines and repeat them with the first group, and so on. It is possible to increase the number of items within the functional capacity limits of working memory through this process called chunking. For example, if you did remember the 10-digit number above, it may be because you spend a lot of time on the telephone. Consequently, your brain automatically chunked the digits into a telephone number format, (491) 508-2637, so that you dealt with three items rather than 10. This chunking process is a way we can increase the functional capacity of working memory. We will discuss more about chunking later in this chapter.

Tip 3.4: Limit Your Talking Points to between Five and Seven Items: Less Is More

Given the limited capacity of working memory, confine your talking points to between five and seven items at any one time. You can limit your number by staying away from items or opinions that are not directly relevant to the content of your presentation. Don't start out saying, "There are 10 things I'd like you to remember about this case." Unless those listening to you can take notes and ask questions, they are already forgetting the earlier items as you move to items eight through 10. This is a case in which less is more.

To some extent, courts are already taking steps to encourage lawyers to limit the information they include in their opening and closing statements. Rule 4-3.4(e) of the Florida Bar, for example, provides that lawyers during trial shall not

> allude to any matter that the lawyer does not reasonably believe is relevant or that will not be supported by admissible evidence, assert personal knowledge of facts in issue except when testifying as a witness, or state a personal opinion as to the justness of a cause, the credibility of a witness, the culpability of a civil litigant, or the guilt or innocence of the accused.

Tip 3.5: Limit Your Presentation Time to between 10 and 15 Minutes: Shorter Is Better

Time Limits of Working Memory. Working memory is a temporary storage area that can deal with items for only a limited time. How long is that time? This intriguing question has been clinically investigated for more than a century. In today's fast-paced world, that time for adolescents and adults is from 10 to 20 minutes. These are average times, and it is important to understand what the numbers mean. An adult normally can process an item in working memory intently for 10 to 20 minutes before fatigue or boredom with that item occurs and the individual's focus drifts. For focus to continue, there must be some change in the way the individual is dealing with the item. As an example, the person may switch from thinking about it to physically using it, or talking about it, or making different connections to other learnings. If something else is not done with the item, it is likely to fade from working memory.

Sometimes, an item can remain in working memory for hours or even days. This is usually a problem that remains unresolved—a question whose answer we seek, or a troublesome family or work decision that must be made. These nagging items can remain in working memory, continually commanding some attention and, if they are of sufficient importance, interfere with our accurate processing of other information. Psychologists call this preoccupation.

As for your presentations, say what is relevant in no more than 15 minutes, less if the material is complicated. Shorter is better. If you have more to say, give your listeners a rest and time to absorb what you have already presented. If appropriate, give them an opportunity to ask questions or make comments.

Long-Term Storage. What factors increase the chances that information will move from working memory to long-term storage for future recall, rather than drop out of the memory system? This is an important consideration because we cannot recall later what we have not stored. Jurors who are constantly asking for parts of a trial transcript to be reread are indicating that they do not clearly remember what they heard.

We cannot recall what we have not stored.

Not all incoming information is processed by the brain with equal attention and speed. Figure 3.10 can help us here. Information that has survival value gets the highest priority and is quickly stored. After all, the brain's main job is to keep you alive. You do not want to have to learn every day that walking in front of a moving bus or touching a hot stove can injure you. The next priority goes to strongly emotional experiences, which also have a high likelihood of being processed quickly and stored permanently. Emotional memories of adverse situations help us to detect and manage difficult and sensitive personal problems that can disrupt the family or social unit. Memories of an enjoyable experience prod us to repeat it so that we can savor the joy once again. Thus, we tend to remember the best and the worst things that happened to us. After survival and emotional data

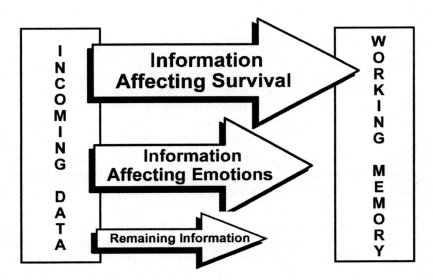

Figure 3.10 Information that affects survival has highest priority, followed by information affecting emotions. The remaining information is then processed.

are processed, we can turn our attention to the remaining information to determine whether it is worth saving.

The Importance of Sense and Meaning

In courtrooms, the listener's (i.e., judge's and jury's) survival and emotional elements are minimal or absent (we hope). So what factors will come into play to determine how much information is remembered? As your presentation is coming to a close, working memory has to decide whether the information you presented is worth storing. It does this by using the listener's past experiences to determine the answers to two critical questions: "Does this information make sense?" and "Does this have meaning?" Imagine the many hours that go into planning your presentations, and it all comes down to these two questions. Let's review them, because at first blush they may seem similar, but in fact they are quite different. "Does this make sense?" This question refers to whether the listener's brain can comprehend your vocabulary and understand the concept on the basis of previously stored experiences. Does it "fit" into what one knows about how the world works? When a person says, "I don't understand," it means the listener is having a problem making sense of what was presented.

"Does it have meaning?" This question refers to whether the item is relevant to the learner. For what purpose should the learner remember it? Meaning, of course, is a personal thing and is greatly influenced by a person's experiences. The same item can have great meaning for one individual and none for another. When someone thinks or says, "Why do I have to know this?" it indicates the person has not, for whatever reason, accepted this information as relevant.

Examples of the Difference between Sense and Meaning

These two examples help to explain the difference between sense and meaning. Suppose you tell a client that the maximum blood alcohol content a person can have before being considered as driving under the influence in his state is 0.08 percent, but it is 0.10 percent in a neighboring state. He can understand this information, so it satisfies the sense criterion. But the percentage in his own state is much more relevant to him, because this is the state in which he will be doing almost all of his driving. Chances are high that he will remember his own state's minimum percentage (because it has both sense and meaning), but will forget that of the neighboring state (it has sense, but lacks meaning).

Let's say you are a lawyer and you read in this morning's newspaper that the average annual salary for dockworkers last year was $52,000,

65

whereas the average salary for lawyers was $94,000. Both numbers make sense to you, but the average lawyer's salary has far more meaning if you are in that profession. If, by chance, you are a lawyer who represents dockworkers, then both salaries would have meaning.

TIP 3.6: Strive for Sense and Meaning

It may seem rather obvious to strive for sense and meaning. Yet, do you remember those times you sat in class as a student and asked yourself: "What is this teacher talking about?" Whenever the listener's working memory decides that an item does not make sense or have meaning, the probability of it being stored is extremely low (see figure 3.11). If either sense or meaning is present, the probability of storage increases significantly (assuming there are no survival or emotional components). But when both sense and meaning are present, the likelihood of long-term storage is very high.

Brain scans have shown that when new learning is readily comprehensible (makes sense) and can be connected to past experiences (has meaning), substantially more cerebral activity is followed by dramatically improved retention.

Meaning Is More Significant. Of the two criteria, meaning has the greater impact on the probability that information will be stored. Think of all the television programs you have watched that were not stored, even

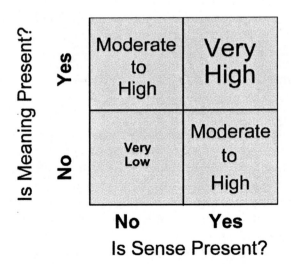

Figure 3.11 The probability of storing information varies with the degree of sense and meaning that are present.

though you spent one or two hours viewing the program. The show's content or story line made sense to you, but if meaning was absent, you just did not save it. It was entertainment, and little or no learning resulted from it. You might have remembered an emotional summary of the show, like whether it was enjoyable or boring, but not the details. On the other hand, if the story reminded you of a personal experience, then meaning was present and you would be more likely to remember details in the program.

> *Meaning isn't inherent in content, but is the result of how the listeners relate it to their past experiences.*

Now think of this process when working with students in a classroom, a client in your office, or others in the courtroom. If you want your listeners to remember what you say, you have to work harder at meaning. Meaning isn't inherent in content, but rather is the result of how your listeners relate it to their own past experiences.

Here are a few ways you can help your listeners attach meaning to what you are presenting.

- Modeling. Models are examples of the new information or concept that the listener can perceive in the courtroom rather than relying on experience. Models can be concrete (an engine) or symbolic (a map). To be effective, a model should—

    (1) Accurately and unambiguously highlight the critical element(s) of the concept;

    (2) Be given early in the presentation when retention is highest; and

    (3) Avoid controversial issues that can evoke strong emotions and redirect the listener's attention.

- Using Examples That Are Likely to Be Part of Your Listeners' Experiences. Find out as much as you can about your listeners' backgrounds and then select examples with which they can identify. This allows your listeners to bring previous knowledge into working memory to accelerate making sense and attaching meaning to the new concept you are presenting. Also, make sure the examples are clearly relevant. This is not easy to do on the spot, so decide on your examples in advance when planning the presentation. There's more later in this chapter on how past experiences affect learning.

TIP 3.7: Keep Your Vocabulary Simple to Help Non-Lawyers Make Sense of What You Say

Albert Einstein once said, "Make things as simple as possible, but no simpler." Don't try to impress your listeners with fancy terminology when simpler words will do. Everyone knows you went to college. Your goal is to be understood. Because jurors cannot ask questions in most jurisdictions while you are presenting, it becomes particularly important that you present material in a clear and logical manner, using vocabulary that non-lawyers will understand. Apparently, even judges will be impressed. According to Bryan Garner in his book, *The Winning Brief*, many judges view lawyers who use legalese as having less prestige and as being less smart than those who are easily understood by non-lawyers.

Here are some ways to avoid legalese.

Instead of saying . . .	Say . . .
aforementioned	(just don't say it)
at this point in time	now
cease and desist	stop
concerning the matter of	about
elucidate	explain
has a negative impact	hurts or harms
in close proximity to	near
in light of the fact that	because
notwithstanding	despite
on a number of occasions	often
owing to the fact that	because or since
procure	get
provision of law	law
render assistance	help
said contract	this contract (use "said" only as a verb: "He said . . . , she said . . .")
subsequent to	after
sufficient number of	enough
the manner in which	how
to the effect that	that
was aware of the fact that	knew

Also, make sure to use all the sensory approaches mentioned earlier that are appropriate. For example, move around the room, use gestures when emphasizing important points, and show diagrams, diagrams, and diagrams that simplify information. It is worth repeating that a picture really is worth a thousand words, especially in today's culture in which so many people have become acclimated to visual messages.

TIP 3.8: Start With the Simplest When Presenting Several Concepts

Have you ever taken a written test in which the first question was very difficult? Your confidence waned and you probably thought: "I'm never going to pass this!" But in tests in which the first questions were easy, you felt more confident about tackling the tougher questions to come. What is the lesson here? Before presenting several different facts or concepts, sort them out, starting with the simplest one and ending with the most difficult. If your listeners are non-lawyers, starting off with a difficult concept may bewilder and lose them. Better to start with the simplest ideas. This way, your listeners gain confidence that they will be able to understand all that you are presenting and thus are more likely to pay attention. Here are a few examples.

Suppose a prosecuting attorney has to explain the concept of money laundering to the jury. This crime contains four basic elements:

(1) The money comes from an unlawful source (e.g., the sale of illegal drugs).

(2) The money is used in a financial transaction (e.g., the money is deposited in a bank account).

(3) The person handling the money knows that its source was illegal.

(4) Something further is done with the money to hide its origin (e.g., the money is used to purchase gold, stocks, monetary instruments, or property).

What should be the order of this presentation, from simplest to most difficult? One possible order is to start with element (1), because this could be substantiated by witness testimony or surveillance techniques. Next follow with elements (2) and (4), because they can be supported by bank and other financial records. Element (3) would be last, because it is the most difficult concept for the jury to comprehend. Essentially, the prosecutor has to convince the jurors to look inside the defendant's mind and be convinced that the defendant had full knowledge that the money resulted from an illegal transaction.

When dealing with a complex case in which the defendant is charged with a long list of crimes, it may be difficult to order them from simplest to most complex. In this instance, you may need to use a different criterion (such as a time line or grouping by categories) to determine the order of your presentation. Remember, after you explain about five to seven items, take a break to give your listeners time to process your information.

TIP 3.9: Remember That Threats and Emotions Affect Memory

Threats and Emotions Affect Memory Processing. We noted earlier that there is a hierarchy of response to sensory input (see figure 3.10). Any input that is of higher priority diminishes the processing of data of lower priority. The brain's main job is to help its owner survive. Thus, data interpreted as posing a threat to the survival of the individual—a burning odor, a snarling dog, or someone threatening bodily injury—are processed immediately.

Because humans are social animals, emotional data also take high priority. When an individual responds emotionally to a situation, the more rational and complex brain processes are suspended. We have all had experiences when anger, fear of the unknown, or immense pleasure quickly overcame our rational thoughts. This override of conscious thought can be strong enough to cause a temporary inability to talk ("I was dumbfounded") or move ("I froze"). This happens because the rational system of the brain is susceptible to stress hormones, which can inhibit cognitive functioning and long-term memory.

Severe trauma, therefore, can actually inhibit one's recall. Although people who have survived a traumatic event say they will never forget it, the fact is they often block it so that recall is difficult. They really do not want to experience it again. In a 2004 study conducted at Yale University, researchers interrogated more than 500 American soldiers who were deprived of food and sleep for 48 hours in mock prison camps. About half of the participants were physically threatened. Twenty-four hours later, most of the soldiers failed to make a positive identification of their interrogators. Those who were physically threatened were the least able to recognize their interrogators. This result suggests that the more intense the trauma, the more the brain blocks painful memories. We remember that we were in a traumatic event, but we do not want to remember the details.

Emotions and Your Client. How a person "feels" about a learning situation determines the amount of attention he or she devotes to it. Emotions interact with reason to support or inhibit learning. The implications of how emotions affect the practice of law are enormous. Let's start with your client. If your client is fearful of bodily harm or emotionally distressed over the legal situation, it will be difficult for you to reason with your client until these fears and emotions subside. You need to focus first on the question of physical protection (survival) and then deal with the emotional issues. Make sure your clients are not getting needlessly upset over something they cannot control.

Emotions in the Courtroom. You can use your own emotional level to affect the emotional state of a witness. To calm a friendly witness, lower the tone and volume of your voice, and speak slower. Keep your distance so that you do not invade the witness's personal space. Conversely, if you want to intimidate a witness you suspect is lying, raise your voice, show anger, and approach the witness at a fast pace with outstretched arms as you ask your question. When the witness's brain senses the threat, the logical processes falter, thereby increasing the possibility of making inconsistent statements during testimony.

> *How a person "feels" about a learning situation determines the amount of attention devoted to it.*

Judges can get emotionally tied up in a case as well, despite their attempts to be objective observers. Getting a judge's emotions to coincide with your own can only be a plus.

What should you do if jurors get too emotionally involved in the case on trial? Are some jurors' eyes tearing up? Do their facial expressions display anger or sadness? These emotions can interfere with the jurors' ability to listen attentively and to process the facts and other important information necessary to deliberate rationally over a verdict. If these emotions are interfering with your planned approach, request a recess to allow time for the emotions to subside. On the other hand, in some instances, you may want emotions to play a role in the jurors' assessment of whether or not the defendant is guilty. In this situation, keep going and let the emotions build.

Moderate your closing statement with emotions. Facts that do not help your case should be stated quickly in a low, monotone voice as you move away from the jury box. Say the points you want the jury to remember in a slow and forceful tone while approaching them. For example, if your client is asking for substantial punitive damages in a negligence case that resulted in pain and suffering, dramatic devices such as catching your breath, sighing, and even getting teary-eyed can have an advantageous impact on judge and jury. Just don't overdo it.

TIP 3.10: Recall That We Remember Best the First and Last Parts of a Presentation

Prime Remembering Times

When the brain is processing new information, the amount that is retained depends, among other things, on when it appears during the presentation. This timing quirk is due in part to the limited capacity of working memory, which we discussed earlier. As new information continues to pour in, working memory must make quick and simultaneous decisions about how to handle each item. This hurried process leads to an interesting phenomenon: At certain time intervals during a presentation, we will remember more than at other intervals.

Let's try a simple activity to illustrate this point. You will need a pencil and a timer. Before you begin, read these instructions. Set the timer to go off in 12 seconds. As you start the timer, you will look at the list of 10 words that follow and try to commit them to memory. When the timer sounds, you will cover the list and quickly write as many of the 10 words as you remember on the lines to the right of the list. Write each word on the line that represents its position on the list (i.e., the first word on line one, the fourth word on line four, etc.). Thus, if you cannot remember the eighth word, but you remember the ninth, write it on line number nine.

Relax now for about a minute. Try to clear your mind of other matters and be prepared to focus only on this task. Ready? Start the timer and stare at the following word list for 12 seconds.

KEF	1. _____
LAK	2. _____
MIL	3. _____
NIR	4. _____
VEK	5. _____
LUN	6. _____
NEM	7. _____
BEB	8. _____
SAR	9. _____
FIF	10. _____

Now cover the list and write the words you remember on the lines to the right. Don't worry if you did not remember all the words. When you are finished, look at the original list again and circle the words that were correct. To be correct, they must be spelled correctly and be in the proper position on the list. Look at the circled words. Chances are you remembered the first 3 to 5 words (lines 1 through 5) and the last 1 to 2 words (lines 9 and 10), but had difficulty with the middle words (lines 6 through 8). Read on to find out why.

The Primacy-Recency Effect. Your pattern in remembering the word list is a common phenomenon that is referred to as the primacy-recency effect. When listening to a presentation (which is a learning episode), we tend to remember best that which comes at the beginning of the session, and remember second best that which comes at the end. We remember least well that which comes just past the middle of the presentation. This is not a new discovery. The early studies on this effect were first published in the 1880s. Later studies helped to explain why this is so. The first items of new information are within the working memory's functional capacity, so they command our attention and are likely to be retained. The later information, however, exceeds the capacity and is lost. As the learning episode concludes, items in working memory are sorted and chunked to allow for additional processing of the arriving final items.

Figure 3.12 shows how the primacy-recency effect influences retention during a 20-minute learning episode. The times are approximate and averages. Note that there are two peaks, each peak representing the degree of greatest retention during that time period. I refer to the first or primary peak as prime-time 1, and the second or recency mode as prime-time 2. Between these two peaks is a time period in which retention during the lesson is least. I call that area the downtime.

This is not a time when no retention takes place, but a time when it is most difficult for retention to occur.

Implications for Your Presentation. The primacy part begins when the listener first focuses on the presenter with the intent to pay attention and to process information (indicated by "0" in figure 3.12). Because this is the time when the greatest retention occurs, present your new information first and take breaks if your

> *When listening to a presentation, we remember best that which comes first, second best that which comes last, and least that which comes just past the middle.*

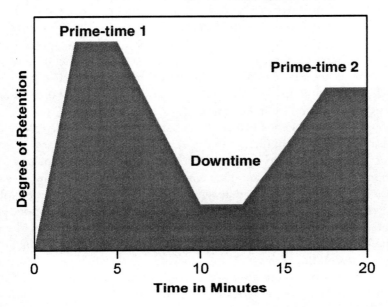

Figure 3.12 The graph shows how the degree of retention varies during a 20-minute learning episode.

presentation is longer than about 15 to 20 minutes.

Implications in the Federal Courts. At the end of trials in federal courts, closing statements are made first by the government's lawyers, followed by the defense lawyer, and then by the government again (for rebuttal). With this format, the defense's closing arguments are in the unfortunate position of being presented during downtime, nestled between the government's two prime-time spots. A defense lawyer in this situation must make a particularly well-organized, compelling, and vivid statement to overcome the drawbacks of presenting during the downtime period.

> *In federal courts, the defense's closing statement is presented during down-time, nestled unfortunately between the government's two prime-time slots.*

74

Overcoming the Downtime Disadvantage. How do you overcome the downtime disadvantage? Remember that the primacy-recency cycle restarts whenever the listener's brain believes new information is coming. Your closing statement, of course, will not contain new information, so you have to find ways to imply that it will. Start with a statement like "I have another way to explain the events that occurred here." If permitted, bring in diagrams, photos, charts, computer information, and almost any tool that presents your position in a new way. Redoing the graphics that you have previously used in this trial can help. Cast them in different colors, vary the typeface, and use different pictures. Keep in motion and repeat vital material with a voice that changes in pitch and tempo. Use phrases such as, "Think about what I just said for a moment." Pause and repeat the point, using different words. Your goal here is to refocus the listeners and to get them to mull over your presentation in a prime-time peak, rather than in the downtime slump.

TIP 3.11: Present New Information First and Do Not Solicit Guesses

New information should be presented first, during prime-time 1, because it is most likely to be remembered. Keep in mind that the listeners will remember almost any information coming forth at this time. It is important, then, that only correct information be presented. This is not the time to be searching for what the listeners may know about something. Don't start your presentation with, "Today, I am going to talk about witness credibility. Does anyone have any idea what that is?" Such a statement encourages listeners to generate ideas about what they think "credibility" is, many of which may be inaccurate or even wrong. Now the listeners have incorrect information taking up valuable (and limited) space in their working memory.

This is definitely not a desirable situation. Present the new material in prime-time 1: "Your decision on whether to believe a witness's testimony can be based on the degree of eye contact, the directness of the responses, the amount of fumbling during responses, and how often the witness redirected the question." Now pause to give the listeners time to process and review during their

> *When you have the listener's attention, present the new information. Don't contaminate prime time with wrong information.*

downtime the information you have just presented. At this point, the information is no longer new, and the mental review helps the listeners organize it for further processing and retention. Repeat important points near the end of your presentation, during prime-time 2. This is the second most powerful learning position and an important opportunity for the listener to find sense and meaning.

Opening Statements. Never waive the opening statement. Get your story out early while the listeners are still mentally fresh. Tell them your plan and what is going to happen. Your goal is to get your listeners to start thinking about the framework you are setting up and how you will complete it. Remember that what you say in prime-time 1 is likely to be remembered, so do not promise in the opening statement something you cannot—or forget to—deliver later on. Remember the 2004 California trial of Scott Peterson, who was accused of murdering his wife and her unborn child? Some legal analysts suggested that a contributing factor to Scott Peterson's guilty verdict was that the jury was miffed because his defense team made promises in their opening statement of exculpatory evidence that never was presented during the trial.

TIP 3.12: Take Breaks in Longer Presentations

Retention Varies with Length of the Presentation. Another fascinating characteristic of the primacy-recency effect is that the proportion of prime-times 1 and 2 to the downtime changes with the length of the presentation. Look at table 3.1. Note that during a 20-minute presentation, the two prime times total about 16 minutes, or about 80 percent of the presentation time. The downtime is about four minutes, or 20 percent of the episode. If we double the length of the presentation to 40 minutes, the downtime increases to about 12 minutes, now up to 30 percent of the total time period. Double it again to an 80-minute episode, and the downtime of 30 minutes takes up almost 38 percent of your presentation time.

TABLE 3.1   AVERAGE PRIME TIMES AND DOWNTIMES

Presentation Time	Prime-Times 1 and 2		Downtime	
	Total Number of Minutes	Percentage of Total Time	Number of Minutes	Percentage of Total Time
20 minutes	16	80	4	20
40 minutes	28	70	12	30
80 minutes	50	62	30	38

As the presentation time lengthens, the percentage of downtime increases faster than for the prime times. Why does this occur? Because the information is entering working memory faster than it can be processed, it accumulates. This cluttering interferes with the sorting and chunking processes and reduces the listener's ability to attach sense and meaning, thereby decreasing retention. Think back to some of those college classes that

> *If your presentation will take more than 30 minutes, break it up into shorter segments.*

lasted for two hours or longer. After the first 20 minutes, did you find yourself concentrating more on taking notes or on learning what was being presented? Perhaps, you lost interest completely.

If your presentation will take more than about 30 minutes, break it up into shorter segments. Ask for a recess, if possible. There is a much higher probability that listeners will remember what you present if you can keep each presentation short and, of course, meaningful. Thus, table 3.1 suggests that presenting two 20-minute segments provides more prime time (approximately 32 minutes) than one 40-minute episode (approximately 28 minutes). These data confirm what we have always suspected: We remember more when presentations are shorter.

TIP 3.13: Be Aware That the Time of Day Affects Attention and Memory

Do you usually feel tired and have difficulty focusing right after lunch? Is this your low-energy point during your day? You are not alone. Most people experience a lull in their energy levels in the early afternoon. It is normal, and it is just one of our body's regular cycles known as circadian rhythms.

Circadian Rhythms. Many of our body functions and their components, such as temperature, breathing, digestion, and hormone concentrations, go through daily cycles of peaks and valleys. These daily cycles are called circadian (from the Latin, "about a day") rhythms. The timing of these cycles is determined by several factors, including hormonal balances, genetic predispositions, and the brain's exposure to daylight. One of these rhythms (called the psychological-cognitive cycle) regulates our ability to focus and process incoming information.

Figure 3.13 shows how our ability to focus and learn changes during the day. Note that we reach our peak ability to focus shortly after we get up in the morning, and we maintain that level for five to six hours. Then it begins to wane, and a trough occurs just past the middle of the day. This is a low point for focus. Learning can still occur during this 20- to 60-minute period, but it requires more mental effort. I have long referred to the trough as the "dark hole of learning." Some cultures recognized long ago how difficult it was to accomplish much learning during this time and established "siesta."

> *Although eating lunch is not the direct cause of the midday cognitive slump, what you eat can affect its duration.*

What causes this trough? We once believed it was due to eating lunch, causing substantial blood flow to be redirected from the brain to the stomach to aid digestion. Recent brain studies, however, show that this trough will occur whether you eat lunch or not. Modern theory holds that the trough is controlled more by fluctuations in the concentration of hormones and neurotransmitters than by your lunch. Nevertheless, what you eat for lunch can affect how long you feel the effects of the trough.

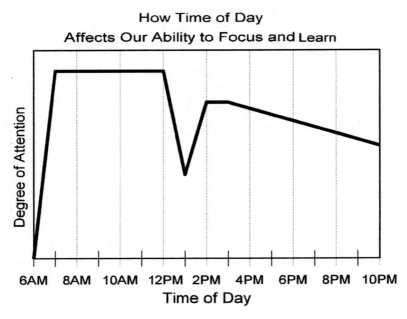

How Time of Day Affects Our Ability to Focus and Learn

Figure 3.13 The chart shows how our ability to focus changes during the course of a day (the psychological-cognitive cycle). Our ability to focus is highest in the morning and lowest just past the middle of the day.

For example, coffee and other caffeinated beverages stimulate the brain, thereby shortening the time in the trough. On the other hand, turkey and whole milk contain l-tryptophan, which is a natural sleep-inducing substance. Eating enough of these two foods for lunch may cause you to feel sluggish and spend more time in the trough than usual. Just hope that the judge and the jurors avoided this particular menu combination at lunch.

TIP 3.14: Make Your Most Important Presentations in the Morning and Try to Avoid the Time Just after Lunch

Implications for Your Presentation. If you want to beat the undesirable effects of the psychological-cognitive cycle's trough, you need to carefully plan in what part of the day you make your important presentations. Most adults can give their fullest attention during the morning hours. This is when they are most likely to focus and, more important, remember what you are saying and showing. Note in figure 3.13 that the degree of attention does increase significantly later in the afternoon. If the morning hours are not available, the afternoon is your second choice to make your presentation.

Try to avoid the 30- to 60-minute period right after lunch when focus is difficult, that "dark hole of learning." If you must present during this time, vary your vocal inflections and the rate at which you speak to avoid a monotone. Walk around the room while speaking so that your listeners are forced to move their heads and stay alert.

If you must present right after lunch, vary your voice, walk around the room, use visuals, and keep it to between 15 and 20 minutes.

Occasionally move closer to your listeners and make eye contact. Be careful, however, that you do not invade their personal space. Some people get apprehensive when strangers get too close, especially in the tense atmosphere of the courtroom. As they deal with this apprehension, they are not paying attention to what you are saying or showing. If possible, use visual aids that are vivid and interesting, and confine your presentation to no more than 15 to 20 minutes. If your listeners start nodding off, request or take a break.

Of course, you can also use the dark hole time to your advantage. For example, if an argument is to be made that can detract from your case, present it in low-key fashion during the dark hole time when the listeners are less likely to remember it.

79

TIP 3.15: Beware of False Memories (Confabulation)
What Is Confabulation?

Have you ever been discussing an experience of many years ago with someone who had shared it with you, and you both started arguing over some of the details? Why does this happen? When we are discussing something from our distant past, long-term memory searches, locates, retrieves, and transfers information related to that experience into working memory. Rote recall, especially of frequently used information, such as your name and address, is simple. These brain pathways are clear and well established, making retrieval time very short. Retrieving more complex and less frequently used concepts, however, is much more complicated. It requires the brain to signal multiple storage sites through elaborate, cluttered, and weaker pathways for intermediate consolidation and ultimate decoding into working memory. It is cumbersome and less accurate for two important reasons. First, most of us do not retain 100 percent of elaborate experiences, such as an extensive vacation. Second, we store parts of the experience in multiple and separate storage areas.

Our brain fabricates information and experiences that we believe to be true.

When retrieving a complicated experience, the long-term memory may not be able to locate all the events being requested, either because of insufficient time or because they were never retained in the first place. Moreover, older memories can be modified or distorted by the acquisition of new and related information. During the retrieval process, memory can unconsciously fabricate the missing or incomplete information by selecting the next closest item it can recall. This process is called confabulation and occurs because the brain is always active and creative, and seems to abhor incompleteness. This is not unlike the way the brain completes visual patterns that do not exist, as in optical illusions. Take a look at figure 3.14. Although you may see a white triangle in the diagram, it does not exist. It is the result of confabulation as the brain seeks to make sense of the pattern.

Confabulation is not lying, because it is an unconscious rather than a deliberate process, and the individual believes the fabricated information to be true. This explains why two people who witnessed the same crime will later recall slightly—or even significantly—different versions

Figure 3.14 The white triangle you may see does not exist. It is a result of confabulation.

of the event. Neither individual stored 100 percent of the experience. If each stored, say, 90 percent, it was not the same 90 percent for both. Their missing and different 10 percent portions will be fabricated and will cause each to question the accuracy of the other's memory. The first witness thinks the robber wore a blue shirt; the next witness says a green shirt. Who should be believed? Worse yet, the less of the experience remembered, the more the brain must fabricate.

Over time, the fabricated parts are consolidated into the long-term memory network. As we systematically recall this memory, minor alterations continue to be made through confabulation. Gradually the original memory is transformed and encoded into a considerably different one that we now believe to be true and accurate. Although we all fall victim to confabulation at one time or another, damage to certain brain areas can cause chronic and extreme confabulation where the recalled memories deviate significantly from reality. The individual is usually unaware of these transformations of memory.

Implications for the Justice System

Confabulation has serious implications for the justice system in that it can be a major impediment when searching for the truth. This tendency for the brain to fabricate information rather than admit its absence can have dire consequences in court trials where eyewitnesses, under the pressure of testifying, feel compelled to provide complete information. Confabulation also raises questions about the accuracy of witnesses recalling very old memories of unpleasant events, such as a childhood accident

> *In the absence of independent verification, it is impossible to decide which events in repressed memory actually occurred and which are the result of confabulation.*

or abuse. Experiments have shown how easy it is to distort a person's recollection of even recent events, or to "implant" memories. In the absence of independent verification, it is impossible to determine which events in the recalled "repressed memory" actually occurred and which events are recalled as the result of confabulation. One can only speculate on the number of defendants who may have been convicted through confabulation for crimes they did not commit.

How Prior Knowledge Affects Learning

The human brain is always trying to make sense of its environment. Whenever new information enters working memory, long-term memory searches storage sites for any past learnings that are similar to, or associated with, the new learning. If the experiences exist, memory networks are activated, and they move information and images into working memory.

The Power of Transfer. The degree to which past learning affects one's ability to acquire new knowledge or skills in another context—such as a lawyer's office or courtroom—describes one phase of the powerful phenomenon called transfer. In other words, we all depend on past learnings to associate with, make sense of, and treat new information. This recycling of past information into the flow not only reinforces stored

> *The more lawyers know about transfer, the more likely they are to use it effectively, rather than become a victim of it.*

information but also aids in assigning meaning to new information. The degree of meaning attributed to new learning will determine the connections that are made between it and other information in long-term storage. Sometimes, of course, what we already know does not help us at all or, even worse, causes confusion over the new learning. Because so much of what lawyers do involves teaching something to another (often a nonlawyer), transfer is an inescapable part of that process. Consequently, the more lawyers know about the power of transfer, the more likely they are to use it effectively in their work, rather than become a victim of it.

Again, I am not trying to make a neuroscientist out of you. But you really need to understand this potent principle of learning. Here's a brief explanation of transfer and how it looms over almost any instructional situation. Generally speaking, transfer occurs either through similarity or association.

Transfer through Similarity. We use transfer when we recall similar items from long-term storage that can assist in learning new information. Transfer is generated by the similarity of the situation in which something is being learned and the situation to which that learning applies. Thus, behavior in one environment tends to transfer to other environments that are similar. For example, commercial jet pilots are first trained in a flight simulator before they sit in the cockpit of a real plane. All the training and learnings they acquired in the simulator (an exact replica of the actual plane) will transfer to the real flying situation. This effect of transfer helps the pilot get accustomed quickly to the actual plane, and it reduces errors.

If you have ever rented a car, you realize that it does not take you very long to get accustomed to it and drive away. The environment is similar to your own car, and most of the important components (steering wheel, dashboard instruments, and floor pedals) are in familiar places. You may need a few moments, however, to locate the windshield wiper controls and light switches.

Lawyers use transfer by similarity in courtrooms when they identify prior cases similar to the one on trial and argue their similarities. Meanwhile, the lawyer for the opposing side may seek to argue the difference(s) between this case and the prior one.

Transfer through Association. Whenever two events, actions, or feelings are learned together, they are said to be associated, or bonded, so that the recall of one prompts the spontaneous recall of the other. The word Romeo elicits Juliet, Hansel recalls Gretel, and Batman gets Robin. A song you hear being played at a mall may elicit memories of some event that is associated with that song. The odor of a cologne once worn by a close friend from the past triggers the emotions of that relationship. Trademarks and product symbols, such as McDonald's golden arches, are designed to recall the product. Although there is no similarity between the two items, they were learned together and, therefore, are recalled together.

Here is a simple example of transfer by association. Look at the list of words that follow. On the lines to the right, quickly write one or two words that come to mind as you read each word in the list. There are no right or wrong answers.

Monday	_____	_____
dentist	_____	_____
Mom	_____	_____
vacation	_____	_____
babies	_____	_____
emergency	_____	_____
money	_____	_____
Sunday	_____	_____

What you wrote down represents thoughts that you have associated with each word in the list. Here are some responses that others have written for Monday: work, blues, quarterback, beginning. For Mom, others have written: love, apple pie, caring, important, security, dad. Were your words anything like these? Maybe they were, or maybe not. Show the list to your family and friends and note their responses. Each of us makes different connections with concepts based on our unique experiences. This activity points out the variety of associations that different people can make with the same thought. Making associations expands our ability to retain information.

> *Making associations expands our ability to retain information.*

Association and Emotions. Transfer by association is particularly powerful when feelings or emotions are associated with a learning. We mentioned earlier that emotions have a higher priority than cognitive processing for commanding our attention. Emotionally loaded words like abortion, Holocaust, and capital punishment often evoke strong feelings. Movies and television can influence people's emotions about events occurring in the world around them. For instance, several recent popular films have depicted big business as greedy and unprincipled (and even murderous). Couple that with the real-life scandals of corporations, such as Enron, Worldcom, and Adelphia, and one can readily understand the public's desire to avenge corporate misdeeds. Consequently, any lawyer representing a large business firm in a court case today has to be concerned about the extent to which anticorporate feelings will taint the jury's judgment.

When you are presenting new information to your listeners, you want to refer to information or experiences in their past that will help them make associations and remember what you are presenting. This is known as positive transfer. At the same time, you want to avoid provoking any experiences and associations they had that could interfere with their understanding of the new information (i.e., negative transfer).

TIP 3.16: Strive for Positive Transfer and Avoid Negative Transfer

Positive and Negative Transfer

Here is an important thing to remember about the inescapable power of transfer: Clients, jurors, judges, other lawyers, and students all have prior knowledge and experiences that will influence their understanding and memory of what you present. If their past learning helps them understand what you are presenting, it is called positive transfer. Sometimes past learning interferes with the listener's understanding of what you are presenting, resulting in confusion or errors. This process is called negative transfer.

Transfer in the Courtroom. Now for an actual example where both positive and negative transfer affected a jury's responsibility to seek the truth (see figure 3.15). The case involved perpetrators using a motor vehicle to stage an accident by deliberately hitting a moving city bus in daylight. Accomplices on the bus complained of serious back and neck injuries and filed claims against the company insuring the city's buses. The insurance company fought the claims in court, saying they were fabricated and excessive. Many of the jurors were blue-collar workers. Chances are that some of them may have had disagreements with insurance companies in the past. As a result, positive transfer encouraged the jurors to see the claimants as "victims," average guys who were trying to collect for their suffering. Meanwhile, negative transfer also played a role by subconsciously suggesting to the jurors that the insurance company, with its deep pockets, was once again trying to avoid paying the little guy. In this instance, the jury sided with the "victims" and awarded them substantial damages despite evidence suggesting that the whole accident was staged.

If you represent the insurance company in a case like this, you have to consider from the outset how to prevent negative attitudes that potential jurors have toward insurance companies from tainting their judgment as they search for the truth. You may be able to search out these negative attitudes during voir dire. During the trial, providing as much proof as possible that the accident was staged can override those feelings of

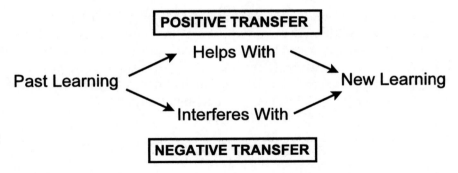

Figure 3.15 Both positive and negative transfer can affect a juror's responsibility to seek the truth.

sympathy for the "victims." Now you can use the jurors' positive transfer for fairness to convert sympathy for the "victims'" sufferings to disdain for the "victims'" deceit.

Another example of negative transfer occurs when an abused female kills her mate out of frustration. The jurors' negative feelings toward domestic abuse can cause them to be more sympathetic to the defendant than to the victim, resulting in a conviction of a far lesser crime, even though the murder was premeditated. Prosecutors in these situations need to focus on the evidence that shows the defendant as a murderer who could have made other choices, such as moving out of the household.

One attorney I interviewed cited an example of using positive transfer with a judge during a juryless trial. The attorney was aware that this particular judge was sensitive about cases in which his rulings were overturned on appeal. The attorney took advantage of this sensitivity by referring in his arguments to some of these overturned cases, even if they did not closely apply to the matter on trial. His hope was that this ploy increased the chances that the skittish judge would rule favorably.

Television Programs and the Burden of Proof. Many non-lawyers realize that in criminal cases the prosecutor bears the burden of proving that the defendant committed a crime beyond a reasonable doubt. Jurors then must decide during deliberations if this burden of proof has been met. What criteria do they use to make that decision? Judges usually address this issue when giving the jury its instructions.

But transfer can play an unsettling role here. We noted earlier that many jurors spend much time watching television, no doubt including those numerous programs that depict courtroom trials. In these dramas, the scenario is often simplistic and the evidence overwhelming. Defendants

86

frequently confess in tears on the witness stand. Nearly everyone is convicted. But these theatrics rarely play out in the real courtroom. Nonetheless, television programs may have formulated or altered a juror's expectation of the burden of proof. It becomes imperative, therefore, that closing arguments and the judge's instructions sufficiently clarify and explain the burden of proof so that jurors can overcome any inaccurate concepts they have acquired from television or any other source.

> *Have television court dramas altered the jurors' understanding of "burden of proof"?*

TIP 3.17: Use Your Listeners' Past Experiences to Help Them Remember

Effect of Past Experiences. Past experiences always influence new learning (transfer). What we already know acts as a filter, helping us attend to those things that have meaning (i.e., relevancy) and discard those that do not. Remember that what is meaningful for you may not be necessarily meaningful for your listeners. How do you get factory workers on a jury to find meaning in the complexities of financial securities law, especially if they keep all their money in banks?

If you expect your listeners to find meaning, you need to be certain that your presentation contains connections to their past experiences, not just yours. Using examples or models helps people attach meaning to topics they otherwise would not find relevant. But you must exercise care. Meaning is so powerful that many states prohibit trial lawyers from using what is dubbed the "golden rule" argument, where the jury is asked: "If you were in this person's situation, what would you have done?"

> *Our past experiences always influence new learning.*

Meaning also helps people remember information by chunking familiar pieces together. Here's a simple example to show that. Get a pencil, paper, and a timer set for 10 seconds. Now stare at the letters below for 10 seconds. Then look away from the page and write them down in the correct sequence and groupings. Ready? Go.

LSDN BCT VF BIU SA

87

Check your results. Did you get all the letters in the correct sequence and groupings? Probably not, but that is okay. Most people do not get 100 percent by staring at the letters in such a short period of time.

Let's try it again. The same rules apply: Stare at the letters below for 10 seconds and write the letters down. Ready? Go.

LSD NBC TV FBI USA

> *Chunking is an effective way to enlarge working memory's capacity and to help the listener make associations that establish meaning.*

How did you do this time? Most people do much better on this example. Now compare the two examples. Note that the letters in both examples are identical and in the same sequence. The only difference is that the letters in the second example are grouped—or chunked—in a way that allows past experience to help working memory process and retain the items. Working memory usually sees the first example as 14 letters plus four spaces (because the grouping is important) or 18 items—much more than its capacity. But the second example is quickly seen as only five understandable items (the spaces no longer matter) and, thus, within the limits of its capacity. Some people may even pair NBC with TV, and FBI with USA, so that they actually deal with just three chunks. These examples show the power of past experience in facilitating memory.

Chunking is an effective way to enlarge working memory's capacity. It can be used to memorize a long string of numbers or words. Most of us learned the alphabet in chunks—for some it may have been abcd, efg, hijk, lmnop, qrs, tuv, wxyz. Chunking reduces the 26 letters to a smaller number of items that working memory is able to handle. Here's an amazing revelation: Although working memory has a functional capacity limit as to the number of chunks it can process at one time, there appears to be no limit to the number of items that can be combined into a chunk. Getting listeners to chunk information can greatly increase focusing, learning, and remembering.

Chunking Strategies. When looking for ways to help you and others chunk information, consider these possibilities.

Advantages and Disadvantages. Categorize the information according to the pros and cons of the concept. Examples include energy use, abortion, and capital punishment.

Similarities and Differences. Compare two or more concepts using attributes that make them similar and different. Examples include comparing the Articles of Confederation to the Bill of Rights, murder to manslaughter, and misfeasance to malfeasance.

Structure and Function. Use these categories when describing concepts that have parts with different functions, such as identifying the parts of a specific medical procedure.

TIP 3.18: Avoid Presenting at the Same Time Two Concepts That Are Very Similar

Presenting two similar concepts at the same time seems so logical. If they are closely related, isn't the listener more likely to remember both? And isn't this the basis for positive transfer? Do similar characteristics of each concept reinforce the learning of the other?

Actually, no. When your brain encodes information from working memory to long-term storage, it labels that memory with a cue that will help you retrieve it later. The cue is like the label on a file folder (see figure 3.16). The more specific the cue that working memory attaches to

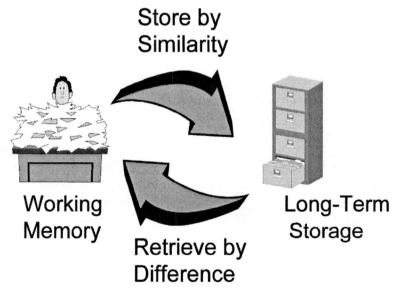

Store by
Similarity

Working
Memory

Retrieve by
Difference

Long-Term
Storage

Figure 3.16 Information is stored in long-term storage by how it is similar to other items within a network. Later, it is retrieved by how it is different from those items.

new information, the easier it is for long-term memory to identify the item when being sought in the future. This process leads to an interesting phenomenon regarding long-term storage and retrieval: We store by similarity, but we retrieve by difference. That is, long-term memory usually stores new learnings in a network that contains learnings with similar characteristics or associations, as perceived by the learner. Thus, "taupe" is stored in the colors network, "anteater" in the animals network, and so forth. But to retrieve an item, long-term memory identifies how it is different from all the other items in that network.

> *We store information by similarity, but we retrieve it by difference.*

Here is a simple example: Let's say you are going to meet some good friends at a crowded football stadium. How do you recognize them? Surely it is not because they each have two arms, two legs, a head, and a torso. These characteristics make them similar to the thousands of others in the crowd. Rather, it is their more subtle differences, such as facial features, walk, and voice, that allow you to distinguish them from everyone else. Your friends' unique characteristics are called their critical attributes. If one of your friends is an identical twin, however, you could have difficulty picking him out from his brother, if both are in the crowd. Similarly, the high degree of similarity between two concepts, coupled with few differences, makes it difficult for a person's memory to tell them apart during recall.

Consequently, whenever two legal concepts have many more similarities than differences, such as excited utterance and spontaneous statement, there is a high risk that the listener cannot tell them apart. In effect, the similarities overwhelm the differences, resulting in the listener attaching the same mental retrieval cues to both concepts. Thus when the listener uses that cue later to retrieve information (as during jury deliberations), the brain could produce either or both concepts, and the learner may not recognize which one is correct. In other words, the very fact that they are so similar can lead to serious retrieval and comprehension problems.

> *When two concepts that are very similar are presented at the same time, confusion may result, unless care is taken to emphasize their difference.*

90

TABLE 3.2 EXCITED UTTERANCE AND SPONTANEOUS STATEMENT	
Similarities	Differences
1. Exceptions to the hearsay rule	1. Amount of time between the startling event and the statement
2. Admissible as evidence	
3. Made under stress	
4. Related to a startling event	

Identifying Concepts That Are Too Similar. You may be asking yourself, "How do I know if two concepts are too similar?" Here's a simple test that will help you answer that question (see table 3.2). Before your presentation, make a list of the similarities and differences between the two concepts. Let's do that using the examples of excited utterance and spontaneous statement.

If the number of similarities and differences is about the same, there is less chance the listeners will be confused. On the other hand, if, as in this example, the number of similarities is far greater than the number of differences (by four to one), confusion is likely. In that situation, try the following:

- Present the Two Concepts at Different Times. Present the first concept, and allow enough time for the listener to accurately and fully consolidate the first concept into long-term storage (usually overnight). Then present the second concept another day.
- Explain the Difference(s) First. Start by explaining the difference(s), or critical attributes, between the two concepts. This works better with less complicated concepts. In the example cited earlier, explain that the only difference between an excited utterance and a spontaneous statement is the amount of time between the event and the statement. A spontaneous statement occurs when it is made as the event is unfolding, such as this one made to a 911 operator: "My husband is coming at me with a knife." An excited utterance comes after the event, such as: "My husband left a few minutes ago, but he tried to kill me with a knife."

Another example is explaining that intent is the only real difference between voluntary manslaughter and involuntary manslaughter: "Did the defendant intend to cause harm to the victim?" Carefully explaining these differences gives the listeners the warnings and the cues they

91

need to separate the two similar concepts and identify them correctly in the future.

Here are some other examples of concepts in law that are similar and could lead to confusion if not presented with care:

- Burden of proof beyond a reasonable doubt (criminal trial) and greater weight (preponderance) of the evidence (civil trial)
- Malicious prosecution and abuse of process
- A concurrent cause and an intervening cause
- The different types of trusts that can be established
- Malfeasance, misfeasance, and nonfeasance
- Arbitration and mediation

TIP 3.19: Use Metaphors to Enhance Transfer

Metaphors are figures of speech that apply a word or phrase to something to which it would not be literally applicable, such as the expressions: food for thought, the brains of the organization, and drowning in money. Metaphors can convey meaning as well and as rapidly as literal language, usually because they are rich in imagery. They are particularly useful in law when explaining a complicated procedure or situation, such as in a medical malpractice case, to those who might not have the background to otherwise understand it.

But metaphors can be misleading. Just think of all the different metaphors that have been used to describe the Internet: an electronic frontier (pioneer metaphor), a never-ending global conversation (telephone metaphor), deliverer of electronic mail (print metaphor), and the information superhighway (library or commercial metaphor). Each of these metaphors generates different images that relate to different bodies of law, and each has its limitations.

Here are a few things to keep in mind when using metaphors in your presentation.

- Select the Metaphor Carefully. Because metaphors are powerful images, it is critical to select the metaphor that will most accurately convey your message. Thus, the criteria for selecting the appropriate metaphor center on goodness of fit (how well the metaphor explains the target concept or process), degree or richness of imagery, and the familiarity that the listeners will have with it. For example, in trying to explain to the jury (in a medical malpractice suit) how putting too much pressure on the umbilical cord can cut off the oxygen supply during the delivery of a fetus, the plaintiff's lawyer likened it to "pinching the hose of a scuba diver, thereby suffocating him." The jury immediately got the image.

- Emphasize the Metaphor Frequently. If the metaphor encompasses your entire concept, it must be emphasized consistently throughout the presentation. The listeners should be alerted to interpret the metaphor figuratively and not literally. One judge told me that she frequently reminds jurors that their task is like solving a jigsaw puzzle. The "pieces" of the puzzle include the evidence, the attorneys' arguments, and her instructions on the law. During deliberations, she tells them, they will participate in a group activity that puts these pieces together to seek the truth, complete the puzzle, and render a verdict.

- Establish the Context. Proper interpretation of the metaphor requires that you establish the context for its use. Metaphors should not be used in isolation, especially if the listeners lack the background to understand them. In a case in which police officers went undercover to catch thugs who were mugging homeless people, the defense lawyer accused the police of entrapment. The officers, he said, tempted the defendants to commit crimes they would otherwise have avoided. The prosecutor established the context for his metaphor by likening the undercover officers to lightning rods that protect a building's occupants from injury during lightning strikes. "These officers merely attracted the evil-doers like lightning rods, thereby protecting the town." The defendants were convicted.

- Provide Instructions for Imagery. Provide the listeners with the instructions they will need to benefit from the rich imagery usually present in metaphors. "Form a mental picture of this" is good advice. A young man on trial for the attempted murder of his father testified that his action was in retaliation for years of sexual abuse he endured from his parent as a young boy. In her closing statement, the defendant's lawyer asked the jury to form a mental picture of what this boy's young life was like: "Imagine being alone in your bedroom at the age of seven, the lights are out, and the door slowly opens. Your father enters, a lurking figure breathing heavily. He begins to stroke your genital area. Think of the fear that runs through this poor boy's heart at that very moment." This vivid metaphor may have been a major reason why the young defendant was convicted of a lesser crime.

- Emphasize Similarities and Differences Clearly. Because the metaphor juxtaposes the similarities of one known object or

93

procedure with another, be sure to emphasize the similarities and differences between the metaphor and the new concept you are presenting. In a motor vehicle negligence case, the defendant had struck a fully occupied van of senior citizens, resulting in many injuries to the passengers. His attorney argued that the plaintiffs should not get higher damages just because they were elderly and thus subject to more injuries than younger passengers. Resorting to metaphor, the plaintiff's attorney likened the situation to crashing into a truckload of eggs, destroying them all at high cost to the farmer. "One can't make the argument that the farmer's truck should have been carrying golf balls."

- Beware of Mixed Metaphors. Because metaphors are such powerful learning devices, make sure you choose them carefully. Mixed metaphors cause confusion and lead to inaccurate recall later.

Chapter 3—Applying Brain Research to Your Practice

Key Points to Ponder

Use this page to jot down key points, ideas, strategies, and resources you want to consider later. This sheet is your personal journal summary and will help to jog your memory.

_____

_____

_____

_____

_____

_____

_____

CHAPTER 4

Putting It All Together

With our new knowledge of the brain, we are just dimly be-
ginning to realize that we can now understand humans, in-
cluding ourselves, as never before, and that this is the greatest
advance of the century, and quite possibly the most significant
in all human history.

—Leslie Hart

The preceding chapters discussed some of the major strides that research
is making in exploring how the brain processes information and learns. I
offered suggestions on how to translate these discoveries into your legal
workplace and practice by using strategies that can improve the efficacy
of your presentations. When planning your presentations, keep the following general thoughts in mind:

- The human brain continually seeks patterns in its search for
  meaning.
- Emotions are an integral part of, and greatly affect, learning,
  retention, and recall.
- Past experiences always affect new learning. Sometimes those
  experiences help acquire new learning (positive transfer); sometimes they interfere (negative transfer).
- The brain's working (temporary) memory has a limited capacity
  of about seven items for most adults.

- Learning style influences the way people process, interpret, and present new information.
- Listeners have to find sense and meaning in new information if they are to remember it.

To help you design effective presentations, I suggest a model framework that consists of seven steps you should consider during your planning. In addition, I propose some important questions you should be asking yourself during planning that relate to the discoveries about the brain discussed throughout the book.

TIP 4.1: Use a Framework Based on Research on Learning to Design Your Presentations

Presentation Design

Nothing beats a good plan. One way to use this neuroscience research effectively is through a framework that forms the basis for your thinking as you plan presentations. On the following pages is a model framework that has been very successful in recent years in helping teachers plan their daily lessons. The model makes explicit those elements that are necessary so that your teaching is more likely to result in learning.

I have modified the model to accommodate presentations commonly made in law practice. Some components of the model are appropriate when working with clients in your office or students in the law classroom, but they are not suitable for a trial or a hearing. The following pages explain the seven components of the model framework, with examples that apply whether working with clients and students or presenting in the courtroom (see table 4.1).

Important Note. Not every presentation needs to include every component. Nonetheless, consider each component during your planning and choose those that are relevant to your objective. For example, in an opening statement at trial, your presentation may focus primarily on objectives (What do I hope to prove to you?) and purpose (Why is that important?). On the other hand, your closing statement, which is a critical review of the case and evidence, would likely include all of the components that are appropriate for the courtroom.

TABLE 4.1. MODEL FRAMEWORK FOR DESIGNING PRESENTATIONS FOR CLIENTS AND STUDENTS OR IN THE COURTROOM	
With Clients and Students	**In the Courtroom**
1. *Focus Strategy.* This opening strategy is designed to capture the listeners' focus. Almost any appropriate technique to get their initial attention can be valuable. To be effective, however, the strategy should— • Allow the listeners to remember an experience that will help them acquire the new information (positive transfer) • Be relevant to your presentation's objective	
Example: "Don't you want to have some control over how your assets will be distributed after you pass away?"	Example: "How do you decide whether to believe what a person is telling you during testimony?"
2. *Presentation Objective.* This is a clear statement of what information the listeners are expected to get out of your presentation.	
Example: "Now I am going to discuss the components of a will."	Example: "Now I am going to discuss the elements you can use to determine the credibility of a witness."
3. *Purpose.* This is a statement of *why* the listeners need to know this information. Whenever possible, it should refer to how the new information is related to other information you may have already presented to these listeners. Remember that past learning always influences new learning. Thus, be aware of what they already know that can help them learn this new information, and what can interfere, as well.	
Example: "You need to know this, because you will remember that I discussed with you the other day the various ways you could apportion your estate for your heirs."	Example: "You will remember that I discussed with you the other day how important it is for you to decide whether a witness is telling the truth. These elements that I am now going to present can help you make that decision, because that is one of your duties as a juror."

TABLE 4.1. MODEL FRAMEWORK FOR DESIGNING PRESENTATIONS FOR CLIENTS AND STUDENTS OR IN THE COURTROOM	
With Clients and Students	**In the Courtroom**
4. *Input.* This is the actual information that the listeners will need to acquire to achieve your presentation objective.	
Example: "Based on your comments, I believe your wishes will best be served by leaving a fixed amount of money to each of your minor children in separate trust funds, setting up a charitable trust for your favorite charity, and leaving the balance of the estate to your spouse."	Example: "You may consider these elements in determining the credibility of a witness: a. the demeanor of the witness while testifying; b. the frankness or lack of frankness of the witness; c. the witness's intelligence; d. any interest the witness has in the outcome of the case; e. the means and opportunity the witness had to know the facts about which the witness testified; f. the witness's ability to remember matters about which the witness testified; and g. the reasonableness of the testimony, considered in light of all the evidence as well as your own experiences and common sense.

TABLE 4.1. MODEL FRAMEWORK FOR DESIGNING PRESENTATIONS FOR CLIENTS AND STUDENTS OR IN THE COURTROOM	
With Clients and Students	**In the Courtroom**
5. **Modeling.** Clear and correct examples will help the listeners make sense of the new information and establish meaning. Be sure that the models you offer are accurate, unambiguous, and noncontroversial. Non-exemplars might be included later to show contrast.	
Example: "Here is an example of a trust format that I generally use for clients with minor children. It stipulates the cash amount and the conditions, such as age and marital status, required to be met before the child can take control of the trust. You can, of course, add other conditions if you wish. I also have an example of a format for a charitable trust. Let's look at the conditions that are common for these types of trusts."	Example: "For example, you might wonder about the credibility of a witness if he or she could get a substantial financial benefit if the defendant is convicted, or if you seriously question how a witness could have possibly known the facts about which that witness testified."

TABLE 4.1. MODEL FRAMEWORK FOR DESIGNING PRESENTATIONS FOR CLIENTS AND STUDENTS OR IN THE COURTROOM	
With Clients and Students	**In the Courtroom**
6. **Check for Understanding.** This refers to the strategies you will use during your presentation to verify that the clients are accomplishing the learning objective. The check is in the form of oral discussion, or any other overt format that convinces you that the objective was achieved. Depending on the results of these checks, you may decide to present some information again, or move on.	Not appropriate for jury trials. However, the verdict form is a useful teaching device. Use an enlargement of the form to guide the jurors through the decision-making process to be sure that they understand their responsibilities. In non-jury trials and appellate hearings, you can ask judges whether your statement was clear, and whether you need to add anything else to clarify the information you presented.
Example: "Just to make sure that I have been clear, let me ask you a few questions to see if you understand the similarities and differences between these types of trusts."	Example: "Let's take a look at the verdict form to make sure you understand each step that needs to be decided during your deliberations."

TABLE 4.1. MODEL FRAMEWORK FOR DESIGNING PRESENTATIONS FOR CLIENTS AND STUDENTS OR IN THE COURTROOM	
With Clients and Students	**In the Courtroom**
7. Closure. In this context, closure does *not* mean ending the session. Rather, this is the time when the minds of the listeners have to summarize their perception of what you presented. You can give specific directions for what the listeners should mentally process and provide adequate time to accomplish it. This is probably the last opportunity the listeners have to attach sense and meaning to the information, both of which are requirements for retention. After you have given the listeners quiet time for mental processing, you can ask them to paraphrase what they learned. In this way, you can assess whether your presentation achieved the intended objective.	Not appropriate for courtroom presentations to solicit questions from jurors. However, in your closing statement, pay attention to the jurors' expressions. If you see a puzzled look, repeat your current point using different words, adding an example or metaphor. Don't forget to thank them for their time, and then lead them to the most important factual or emotional point you want them to remember. This is, after all, prime-time 2!
Example: "These are very important decisions you will be making. Take a few minutes to think over what I have shown and explained to you to see if it makes sense. When you are ready, tell me in your own words the conditions you will set forth in the trusts for your minor children and for your favorite charity."	Example: "It is very clear that there was malice aforethought. [Puzzled look on jurors' faces] By that I mean, the defendant took time to plan this crime long before he committed it. That's the most important thing for you to remember in this case."

103

TIP 4.2: Ask Yourself These Important Questions When Planning Your Presentations

Important Questions to Ask During Planning. Table 4.2 contains some important questions to ask yourself while planning your presentations, the rationale for asking them, and the corresponding tips that explain the rationale.

TABLE 4.2 *IMPORTANT QUESTIONS TO ASK WHEN PLANNING PRESENTATIONS*		
Question	*Rationale*	*See Tip*
1. Am I remembering my own learning style preferences when planning this lesson?	Your own preferences will influence the information you select, and how you present it.	1.2, 1.3, 1.4, 3.1
2. Do I need to do anything special because of the time of day when I am making this presentation?	Most people learn and remember best in the morning and least well just past the middle of the day.	3.13, 3.14
3. Have I included activities that are multisensory?	Using many senses increases retention.	3.1
4. What strategies am I using to help the listeners find meaning in the information?	Meaning helps retention.	3.2, 3.6
5. What visual aids can help this presentation?	Visual aids help hemispheric integration and retention.	3.3
6. Am I limiting the number of items I present at any one time to about five?	Working memory has a limited capacity.	3.4
7. Am I using the two prime times to the best advantage, that is, by putting the most important information first and last?	Maximum retention occurs during the prime times at the beginning and end of a presentation.	3.5, 3.10, 3.11
8. What will the listeners be doing during downtime?	Minimum retention occurs during downtime.	3.5, 3.12

Question	Rationale	See Tip
TABLE 4.2 *IMPORTANT QUESTIONS TO ASK WHEN PLANNING PRESENTATIONS*		
9. What chunking strategies are appropriate for this objective?	Chunking increases the number of items working memory can handle at one time.	3.6
10. Have I selected vocabulary that the listeners can easily understand, and am I explaining technical terms?	Legal jargon may be misinterpreted by listeners who are not lawyers.	3.7
11. Have I sequenced the information to start with the simplest and end with the most difficult?	Starting with the simplest information gives listeners confidence that they will understand your presentation.	3.8
12. What emotions need to be considered or avoided when presenting this objective?	Emotions play a key role in a listener's acceptance and retention of learning.	3.9
13. Have I divided my presentation into segments of about 15–20 minutes each?	Short segments have proportionally less downtime than longer ones.	3.10
14. What prior information and experiences do the listeners possess that will help or interfere with them understanding the new information?	Prior knowledge and experiences strongly influence new learning.	3.15, 3.16, 3.17
15. Am I presenting at the same time concepts that are too similar to each other?	Concepts that are too similar can be confused and, thus, should not be taught together.	3.18
16. Would using a metaphor better explain this information?	Metaphors enhance transfer, hemispheric integration, and retention.	3.19

TIP 4.3: Beware the Dangers of Success

Conscientious leaders in all professions want to be successful. But success can also spoil a leader. People can get so wrapped up in their past successes that they begin to stall and can no longer sustain the innovative thinking and creative energy they once had that made their law firm, courtroom, or classroom so impressive. More often than not, these leaders do not recognize that this is happening. On the contrary, in their minds, they are doing as well as ever. They fail to realize that they are slowly becoming supporters of the status quo. How does this happen? Mainly because—

> *Those who rest on their laurels are wearing them at the wrong end.*

- Leaders interpret and evaluate the modern-day events in terms of their past successes. When people focus too much on their past successes, these memories dominate the working memory area of the brain, thereby limiting the amount of memory available to concentrate on the present.

Because memories of the past are more comforting than the problems of the present, all new events are colored by the past. Although it is normal for the brain to interpret new situations in light of past experiences (remember transfer?), those who concentrate on past successes fail to see new trends and patterns that may be emerging in the present. As they cling more to the past, some leaders begin to interpret innovations as a threat. Those who rest on their laurels are wearing them at the wrong end.

- Thought processes of leaders become hardwired in their brain to form a network that acts as a filter of new information. The successful thinking and problem-solving routines that leaders have used in the past eventually get hardwired in the brain and become almost automatic. This automatic response may seem desirable, but it can also be a drawback because leaders miss many opportunities to detect new patterns. They get caught within their own stereotypic thinking paradigm and avoid challenging their previously held beliefs.
- Leaders lose their sense of naïveté and humility, become egotistical, and begin to value only their own opinions. Leaders who have had a string of successes with no failures in between are particularly vulnerable to becoming egotistical. They believe

106

they know and do their job well and may close their minds to new ideas. If they stay in one organization too long, they get comfortable and complacent and less willing to disturb their environment with innovation. Trial lawyers who have seldom lost a case, and judges who have been consistently upheld on appeal, can get overly confident and lose the edge that made them so prominent.

Leaders should watch for signs that they may be falling into any of these three routes to failure. When they talk too much about past successes, rely too heavily on instinctive problem-solving strategies, and feel overly comfortable in their position, it is time for them to stretch into unfamiliar domains.

Chapter 4—Putting It All Together

Key Points to Ponder

Use this page to jot down key points, ideas, strategies, and resources you want to consider later. This sheet is your personal journal summary and will help to jog your memory.

_____

_____

_____

_____

_____

_____

_____

APPENDIX

Basic Brain Facts

No other known entity in the universe is as complicated and as fascinating as the human brain. This three-pound mass of hundreds of billions of nerve cells is intricately organized to control our feelings, behavior, and thoughts. It collects and sorts information, learns complex skills, masters spoken language, stores the memories of a lifetime, and contains the secret of ourselves. For centuries, scientists have been attempting to understand exactly how the brain grows and develops into this amazing organ.

Until recently, their efforts were thwarted by the reality that the brain could be examined physically only in autopsy. Microscopic and macroscopic sections of brain tissue gave clues about structure but not function. Today, however, brain imaging technologies have given neuroscientists powerful new tools to look at brain structure and function in living persons. Computed tomography (CT scans, also called CAT scans), positron-emission tomography (PET scans), and functional magnetic resonance imaging (fMRI) are especially helpful in deciphering the complex cerebral structures and processes involved in language acquisition, problem solving, and higher-order thinking.

In addition to the imaging techniques, advanced systems monitor and record the electrical signals (electroencephalography, or EEG) as well as the magnetic fields (magnetoencephalography, or MEG) that are produced when electrical impulses travel within brain cells, called neurons. These recordings are valuable in localizing the source of signals originating in brain regions as small as one cubic millimeter (about the volume of a poppy seed) of cerebral cortex, and in timing any changes to the nearest thousandth of a second. This new technology allows scientists to determine which parts of the brain are most active while doing certain tasks, such as speaking, reading, solving problems, or getting emotionally excited.

Basic Brain Structures

To understand the complexity of the human brain, we will first look at the major parts of the outside of the brain (see figure A.1). Three major

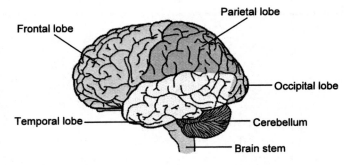

Figure A.1 This diagram shows the location of the brain's four lobes as well as the cerebellum and the brain stem.

structures are visible: the cerebral hemispheres composed of the four lobes of the cerebrum, the cerebellum, and the brain stem.

The Cerebrum. The cerebrum makes up the largest part of the brain (about 85 percent by weight). Its surface is highly convoluted and covered with a laminated sheet of six layers of cells approximately two millimeters (about one-tenth of an inch) in thickness. The convolutions allow a great deal more of this laminated sheet (called the cerebral cortex) to be packed into the confines of the human skull. Although the minor wrinkles are unique in each brain, several major folds are common to all brains. In the largest part of the brain, the major folds define a set of four lobes (called the frontal, temporal, occipital, and parietal), each of which specializes in performing certain functions.

Frontal Lobes. Often referred to as the executive control center, the frontal lobes contain almost 50 percent of the volume of the cerebrum. The area at the very front of these lobes (i.e., just behind the forehead) is called the prefrontal cortex, which is believed to be the site of our personality, curiosity, decision making, and ability to reflect on the consequences of our actions. Curbing the excesses of our emotions is another of the prefrontal cortex's important functions.

Most of the working memory is located in the frontal lobes, so this is the area where focus occurs. The frontal lobes, however, mature slowly. Brain scan studies of postadolescents reveal that the frontal lobes continue to mature into early adulthood, probably until the age of 22 to 24. Thus, the emotional regulation capability of the frontal lobes is not fully operational during adolescence. This is one reason why adolescents and young adults are more likely than older adults to submit to their emotions and resort to high-risk behavior.

Temporal Lobes. The temporal lobes are the speech center. They are involved in the interpretation of sound, speech (primarily on the left side), and some aspects of long-term and visual memory.

Occipital Lobes. Located across the rear of the brain, the main function of the occipital lobes is visual processing.

Parietal Lobes. The parietal lobes are primarily concerned with attending to stimuli, sensory integration, and orientation.

A deep fissure running from front to back divides the cerebrum into two hemispheres. For some still unexplained reason, the nerves from the left side of the body cross over to the brain's right hemisphere, and those from the right side of the body cross over to the left hemisphere. The two hemispheres are connected by a thick cable that allows the hemispheres to communicate with each other and to coordinate activities.

The Cerebellum. The cerebellum (Latin for "little brain") coordinates every movement. Because the cerebellum monitors impulses from nerve endings in the muscles, it is important in the learning, performance, and timing of complex motor tasks, such as speaking. The cerebellum also may store the memory of rote movements, such as touch-typing, tying a shoelace, and playing a musical instrument. A person whose cerebellum is damaged cannot coordinate movement and has difficulty with speech.

The Brain Stem. The oldest and deepest area of the brain, the brain stem is often referred to as the reptilian brain, because it resembles the entire brain of a reptile. Here is where vital body functions (respiration, body temperature, blood pressure, and digestion) are monitored and

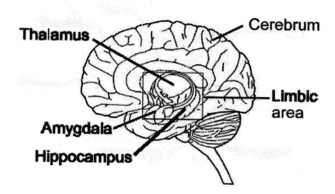

Figure A.2 This cross section shows the cerebrum as well as the main components of the brain's limbic area.

111

controlled. The brain stem also houses the systems that play an active role in sleeping, waking, and attending to survival messages.

Next, we look at the inside of the brain and at some of its major structures (see figure A.2) located in the emotional or limbic area of the cerebrum.

The Limbic Area. Above the brain stem lies the limbic area, most of whose structures are duplicated in each hemisphere of the brain. This area regulates fear and other aspects of emotional memory. Some parts of the limbic area process and interpret specific sensory information, but the three parts of the limbic area important to learning and memory are the following:

Thalamus. This structure is the brain's switching station. All incoming sensory information (except smell) goes first to the thalamus for preliminary processing and integration. From here it is directed to other parts of the brain for additional processing.

Hippocampus. Derived from the Greek word for a sea monster resembling a seahorse, because of its shape, the hippocampus hugs the inside of the temporal lobe. It plays a major role in consolidating learning and in converting information from working memory via electronic signals to the long-term storage regions, a process that takes from days to months. The hippocampus constantly checks information relayed to working memory and compares it to stored experiences. This process is essential for the creation of meaning.

Amygdala. Attached to the front end of the hippocampus, the amygdala (Greek for "almond") plays an important role in emotional behavior, especially the fear response. It regulates those interactions that are necessary for the organism's survival, such as whether to fight or flee, to eat or not eat, and when to mate. Because of its proximity to the hippocampus and its activity on PET scans, researchers believe that the amygdala encodes an emotional message, if one is present, whenever an experience is destined for long-term storage. Apparently, these memories can be established even unconsciously. This explains why we tend to remember vividly the best and the worst things that happen to us.

Brain Cells. The activities of the brain are carried out by signals traveling along brain cells. The brain is composed of more than a trillion cells of at least two known types: nerve cells and their support cells. Nerve cells are called neurons, and represent about one-tenth of the total number of cells—roughly 100 billion. Most of the remaining cells are the support cells, called glial (Greek for "glue") cells, that hold the neurons together, act as filters to keep harmful substances out of the neurons, and moderate the speed of neural signals.

112

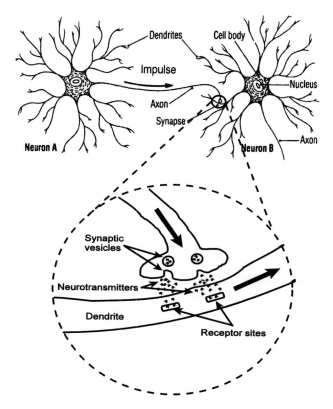

Figure A.3 Brain cells, called neurons, transmit signals along an axon and across the synapse to the dendrites of a neighboring cell.

Neurons are the functioning core for the brain and the entire nervous system. They come in different sizes, depending on their location in the body. Brain cells are small; about 30,000 of them could fit on the head of a pin. Unlike other cells, the neuron (see figure A.3) has tens of thousands of branches or dendrites (Greek for "tree") emerging from its center. The dendrites receive electrical impulses from other neurons and transmit them along a long fiber, called the axon (Greek for "axis"). Each neuron has a cell body and only one axon.

Neurons have no direct contact with each other. Between each dendrite and axon is a small gap of about a millionth of an inch called a synapse (Greek for "to join together"). This system allows for maximum flexibility. Because the neurons are not physically tied to each other, neuron-to-neuron interactions can form, reform, and dissolve from one moment to the next. This flexibility accounts for the brain's plasticity and explains why learning continues to occur during our entire lifetime.

Signals generated within neurons are electrical, but communication between neurons is chemical. The neuron sends out spikes of electrical activity through the axon to the synapse where the activity releases chemicals stored in sacs (called synaptic vesicles) at the end of the axon. The released chemicals, called neurotransmitters, travel across the synapse to a receptor site and either excite or inhibit the neighboring neuron. More than 50 different neurotransmitters have been discovered so far. Some of the more common neurotransmitters are dopamine, glutamate, acetylcholine, epinephrine, and serotonin. Some neurotransmitters, such as glutamate, are found everywhere in the brain; others, like dopamine, are restricted to certain regions.

Brain Size and Intelligence. The idea that a relationship exists between brain or head size and intelligence has long been the subject of controversy. Popular in the nineteenth century, the concept seemed to make sense: the more brain, the more intelligence. Although early-twentieth-century biologists ridiculed the idea, modern brain imaging studies actually show a small positive correlation between brain volume and intelligence. In one study conducted in 2001, researchers used MRI to scan the brains of 20 pairs of identical and fraternal twins. The researchers gave the subjects intelligence tests and found that intelligence (as measured by these tests) was significantly linked with the amount of brain matter in the frontal lobes.

The results surprised the researchers who found it hard to believe that something as simple as frontal lobe brain volume affects something as complex as intelligence. Nonetheless, it could be that the larger the brain cell mass, the greater the number of cell-to-cell connections. What still remains a mystery is whether the larger cell volume was the cause of higher intelligence or the other way around—people with strong motivation might use their brains more and thus develop a higher density of neurons. The researchers cautioned, however, that because this study involved collective data, the size of brain volume in the frontal lobes cannot be used to measure the intelligence of an individual.

Answer to the Creativity Puzzle (Figure 1.1)

Recall that the task was to draw four lines through the nine dots without lifting the pencil, and without going through any point more than once. This can be accomplished only if the lines extend beyond the virtual square outlined by the dots. Many people feel confined to that square even though that restraint is not stated in the directions. How did you do?

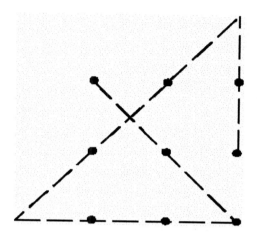

GLOSSARY

Amygdala. The almond-shaped structure in the limbic area of the brain that encodes emotional messages to long-term storage.

Axon. The long and unbranched fiber of a neuron that carries impulses away from the cell to the next neuron.

Brain stem. The part of the brain that receives sensory input and monitors vital functions such as heartbeat, body temperature, and digestion.

Cerebellum. One of the major parts of the brain, it coordinates muscle movement.

Cerebrum. The largest of the major parts of the brain, it controls sensory interpretation, thinking, and memory.

Chunking. The ability of the brain to perceive a coherent group of items as a single item or chunk.

Circadian rhythm. The daily cycle of numerous body functions, such as breathing and body temperature.

Closure. The teaching strategy that allows learners quiet time to mentally reprocess what they have learned during a lesson.

Confabulation. The brain's replacement of a gap in long-term memory by a falsification that the individual believes to be correct.

Corpus callosum. The bridge of nerve fibers that connects the left and right cerebral hemispheres and allows communication between them.

Cortex. The thin but tough layer of cells covering the cerebrum that contains all the brain cells used for cognitive and motor processing.

Critical attributes. Characteristics that make one concept unique from all others.

Dendrite. The branched extension from the cell body of a neuron that receives impulses from nearby neurons through synaptic contacts.

Endorphins. Opiate-like chemicals in the body that lessen pain and produce pleasant and euphoric feelings.

Frontal lobes. The front part of the brain that monitors higher-order thinking, directs problem solving, and regulates the excesses of the emotional (limbic) system.

Glial cells. Special cells in the brain that surround each neuron and provide support, protection, and nourishment.

Hemisphericity. The notion that the two cerebral hemispheres are specialized and process information differently.

Hippocampus. A brain structure that encodes information from working (temporary) memory to long-term storage.

Imagery. The mental visualization of objects, events, and arrays.

Immediate memory. A temporary memory for which information is processed briefly (in seconds) and, subconsciously, is then either blocked or passed on to working memory.

Limbic system. The structures at the base of the cerebrum that control emotions.

Long-term storage. The areas of the cerebrum where memories are stored permanently.

Negative transfer. When past learning interferes with the acquisition of new learning.

Neuron. The basic cell making up the brain and nervous system, consisting of a globular cell body, a long fiber called an axon that transmits impulses, and many shorter fibers called dendrites that receive them.

Neurotransmitter. One of more than 50 chemicals stored in axon sacs that transmit impulses from neuron to neuron across the synaptic gap.

Occipital lobes. Located at the back of the cerebrum, the occipital lobes are primarily responsible for processing visual information.

Parietal lobes. These lobes are located in the upper rear portion of the cerebrum and are primarily concerned with attending to stimuli, sensory integration, and orientation.

Plasticity. The brain's lifelong ability to continually change in structure in response to new situations.

Positive transfer. When past learning helps in the acquisition of new learning.

Primacy-recency effect. The phenomenon whereby one tends to remember best that which comes first in a learning episode and second best that which comes last.

Prime time. The time in a learning episode when information or a skill is more likely to be remembered.

Rehearsal. The reprocessing of information in working memory.

Retention. The preservation of learning in long-term storage in such a way that it can be identified and recalled quickly and accurately.

Synapse. The microscopic gap between the axon of one brain cell and the dendrite of another.

Temporal lobes. Located on each side of the cerebrum, the temporal lobes focus mainly on language and music comprehension, hearing, smell, and taste.

Thalamus. A part of the limbic system that receives all incoming sensory information, except smell, and shunts it to other areas of the cortex for additional processing.

Transfer. The influence that past learning has on new learning, and the degree to which the new learning will be useful in the learner's future. See also negative transfer and positive transfer.

Working memory. The temporary memory wherein information is processed consciously.

RECOMMENDED READING

Edelman, G. (2007). *Second Nature: Brain Science and Human Knowledge.* New Haven, CT: Yale University Press.

Fine, C. (2008). *A Mind of Its Own: How Your Brain Distorts and Deceives.* New York: W. W. Norton.

Garland, B. (2004). *Neuroscience and the Law.* Washington, DC: Dana Press.

Gazzaniga, M. S. (1998). "The Split Brain Revisited." *Scientific American* (July): 48–55.

Goertz, J. (2000). "Creativity: An Essential Component for Effective Leadership in Today's Schools." *Roeper Review* 22: 158–162.

Goldberg, E. (2001). *The Executive Brain: Frontal Lobes and the Civilized Mind.* New York: Oxford University Press.

Hawkins, J., and S. Blakeslee. (2004). *On Intelligence.* New York: Times Books.

Hirstein, W. (2006). *Brain Fiction: Self-Deception and the Riddle of Confabulation.* Cambridge, MS: The MIT Press.

Jausovec, N. (2000). "Differences in Cognitive Processes between Gifted, Intelligent, Creative, and Average Individuals while Solving Complex Problems: An EEG Study." *Intelligence* 28: 213–240.

Korol, D. L., and P. E. Gold. (1998). "Glucose, Memory, and Aging." *American Journal of Clinical Nutrition* 67: 764S–771S.

Quartz, S., and T. Sejnowski. (2002). *Liars, Lovers, and Heroes: What the New Brain Science Reveals about How We Become Who We Are.* New York: Morrow.

Restak, R. (2003). *The New Brain: How the Modern Age Is Rewiring Your Mind.* New York: Rodale.

Sousa, D. A. (2007). *How the Brain Learns,* 3rd edition. Thousand Oaks, CA: Corwin Press.

Sousa, D. A. (2003). *The Leadership Brain: How to Lead Today's Schools More Effectively.* Thousand Oaks, CA: Corwin Press.

Zeki, S., and O. Goodenough, eds. (2006). *Law and the Brain.* New York: Oxford University Press.

INDEX